Earn It!

Earn It!

What to Do When Your Kid Needs an Entitlement Intervention

Michael G. Wetter, PsyD,
and Eileen Bailey

Hazelden
Publishing

Hazelden Publishing
Center City, Minnesota 55012
hazelden.org/bookstore

ISBN: 978-1-61649-717-0

Library of Congress Cataloging-in-Publication Data is on file with the
Library of Congress.

Editor's note
The names, details, and circumstances may have been changed to protect
the privacy of those mentioned in this publication.

This publication is not intended as a substitute for the advice of health
care professionals.

Readers should be aware that the websites listed in this work may have
disappeared or changed between when this book was written and when
it is read.

21 20 19 18 17   1 2 3 4 5 6

Acquiring editor: Vanessa Torrado
Developmental editor: Mindy Keskinen
Production editor: Victoria Tirrel
Cover and interior design: Terri Kinne

Eileen

In loving memory of my son
Frederick (Derek) C. Harris III
1985–2017
You shall forever remain in my heart

Michael

To my daughter Leah Brielle Wetter
The constant light in my life who
brightens each and every day
You are my sunshine

Contents

Take an Honest Look

Do you remember the Dursley family of Harry Potter fame? If ever there was an entitled child, it would be Harry's cousin Dudley, who was just turning eleven in *Harry Potter and the Sorcerer's Stone*. In this scene, Harry and the Dursleys are gathered at the breakfast table on Dudley's birthday.

> Dudley, meanwhile, was counting his presents. His face fell. "Thirty-six," he said, looking up at his mother and father. "That's two less than last year."
>
> "Darling, you haven't counted Auntie Marge's present, see, it's here under this big one from Mummy and Daddy."
>
> "All right, thirty-seven then," said Dudley, going red in the face. Harry, who could see a huge Dudley tantrum coming on, began wolfing down his bacon as fast as possible in case Dudley turned the table over.
>
> Aunt Petunia obviously scented danger too, because she said quickly, "And we'll buy you another two presents while we're out today. How's that, popkin? Two more presents. Is that all right?" . . . Uncle Vernon chuckled. "Little tyke wants his money's worth, just like his father. 'Atta boy, Dudley!" He ruffled Dudley's hair.

If you're a young parent today, you might have grown up with J.K. Rowling's instant-classic series. Maybe you eagerly waited for each new book and its eventual movie adaptation. Or if your kid is already a teen or young adult, maybe they were the ones eagerly waiting for Harry Potter's next adventure.

If you missed the Harry Potter boat altogether, you might recall the kids trailing Willy Wonka through his candy wonderland in the movie based on Roald Dahl's *Charlie and the Chocolate Factory*. Aside from our hero, Charlie, all the kids get their comeuppance: greedy Augustus Gloop, spoiled Veruca Salt, "me-first" Violet Beauregarde, and screen-addicted Mike Teevee.

We laugh at the fates of those four super-presumptuous kids, at Dudley the indulged birthday boy, and at the parents who enable them. But if we're parents ourselves, is our laughter just a bit anxious? Do we see traces of these characters in our own kids? All of these fictional children give us an object lesson in entitlement. And the message to parents is, don't let this happen on your watch.

Whether your kid is a toddler, school age, teen, or young adult, you're concerned about entitled attitudes—and *Earn It!* is for you. Yes, Dudley and his fictional kind are totally over the top. But they embody a very recognizable human tendency—the wish to slack off, to be catered to, to take more than we give. Most parents today are aware that kids can easily develop entitled attitudes, and it takes some intentional parenting to keep our kids on track.

Parents want to raise self-confident children, kids with a can-do attitude who are eager to use their skills, learn, and grow. But what about children who think they "can do" whatever they feel like doing, anytime? What about teens who feel entitled to act on their whims with little regard for others? If you're a parent who sees those attitudes in your own kid sometimes—or if you want to help prevent them right from the start—you've come to the right place.

This book is a guide to recognizing patterns of entitlement in your family life—because that's what they are: *family* patterns. Although it might be tough to admit it, yes, maybe your child does act a bit spoiled at times. The good news is, you can take steps toward changing those patterns. And guess what? It starts with you. As you change yourself, your child, and your family culture, you'll find that you'll all be better equipped for a responsible, satisfying life.

So what's the difference between self-confidence and entitlement? People with a healthy sense of confidence have a feeling of competence and belonging. Their self-awareness includes an accurate sense of their goals, wants, and needs. If they've worked hard to attain a goal, they probably feel satisfied and perhaps even entitled to a reward, even when that reward is simply enjoying the accomplishment. That kind of entitlement is legitimate; they've *earned* that reward.

But people with entitled attitudes feel that they deserve rewards even if they've done nothing to earn them. In fact, this is a *false* sense of entitlement (you might have heard the term *me-centric*). You might recognize it in children who demand the newest toy or designer clothes, and whose parents oblige out of guilt or fatigue. Or you might notice that your own kid expects you to cook, clean, do their laundry, and run them to sports or social events, but they balk every time you ask them to pick up their toys or empty the dishwasher.

Entitlement is often confused with the word *affluenza*, a term used to describe the spoiledness of the very rich. But entitlement occurs across all income groups. It's a state of mind, the concept that "I *deserve*, even without putting in an effort."

This attitude begins at home, but often our society helps reinforce it. Think of the so-called participant trophies given to *all* kids playing on a sports team—not just those who excel. Advocates of these awards say they boost kids' confidence and self-image (these trophies appeared along with the "self-esteem movement" starting in the 1970s). But others say we shouldn't reward children just for showing up. In competitive settings, some say, we should honor success and the effort that went into it. More on this subject later. But the question remains: by trying to foster self-confidence, have we instead fostered a sense of entitlement?

Me-first attitudes can seep into every aspect of life. Children who believe they're entitled to have everything go their way find it hard to cope when things don't. As preschoolers, they might have frequent temper tantrums. Later, they might lash out at classmates for real or perceived slights. They might be difficult to live with, defiantly ignoring requests to do chores or homework because they want to play video games. They might whine, cry, or become belligerent when forced to share, or when their parents refuse to let them stay up a little later.

And these kids often turn into adults who feel entitled. College professors have noticed it: students demand to make up a test because they overslept, or they expect an A for showing up to class consistently, even when they didn't put forth much effort. The workplace isn't much different. When these young adults enter the workforce, they may expect to start with salaries higher than their experience or qualifications warrant. They want raises or promotions before they are deserved, and they blame those around them—their coworkers or their boss—when things don't go their way. They become selfish and demanding partners and friends, and wonder why no one wants to be around them. Like entitled kids, entitled adults see only *their* needs as important.

Over time, entitlement can also play a role in substance use and addiction. Pampered kids develop a false sense of control, since they call the shots in their own families. And this kind of entitlement can also lead to a false sense of being able to control one's use of alcohol or drugs. This false sense of control can lead to pervasive use. It's a similar mindset: alcoholics believe they *deserve* a drink because they had a hard day or because they're celebrating a success. They don't see that their drinking affects others in their families. Beyond alcohol and drugs, we see this same attitude in behavioral addictions, such as pornography and gambling. The addict's needs become all-important and supersede other people's needs. Family members frequently end up rearranging their lives to meet the needs of the addict.

So we can see how early prevention of entitled attitudes can help *lower* our kids' risk of future addiction, but of course, it's no guarantee. Many other factors—genetic, neurological, and environmental—are involved in addiction and recovery. But it's one more reason the costs of entitled attitudes can be so high. And for the person who does become addicted, some experts also see a sense of entitlement as a potential roadblock to recovery. The addict may give up the substance of choice, but unless they address their entitlement issues, the chances of relapse are higher.

So the stakes are high, but so are the odds for meaningful change—if you take action as a parent. Whether you notice signs of entitlement in your toddler, your grade-schooler, your teen, or your adult child, there are steps you can take to change your thinking and your family dynamics. Your family life will have less tension and more consistency. You might find that family members have more room to actually enjoy each other's company!

This book has two sections. In **Part 1: Entitlement Is a Family Dynamic,** you'll learn the basics: what is entitlement, and what exactly is at stake? Chapter 1 digs into those questions and gives you some red flags that show entitlement patterns in your child's behavior and in your own parenting habits. Chapter 2 reveals entitlement as a family dynamic—one that you can change, starting with your own perceptions and behaviors. You'll learn three ways you can start changing right now by laying the groundwork to shift your family culture. In chapter 3, we'll discuss how societal norms can reinforce me-first attitudes, and you'll learn new ways to approach consumerism, advertising, and social media with your child. In chapter 4 we'll talk about the future: how child entitlement often plays out in adulthood, and the importance of turning the tide now. Read part 1 in full for a complete view of all the factors at play.

Part 2: Change Yourself, Change Your Child is your toolbox. Read chapter 5 in full: that's where you start to truly change yourself. Chapters 6 through 15 address particular habits of thought and areas of daily life where entitled attitudes show up, and explore how to shift them. Cultivating respect, gratitude, and kindness; handling chores and allowances; making decisions and managing feelings; learning how to give back—these chapters can be read in any order (and referred to as necessary). In chapter 16, we'll discuss how to work together with other influencers in your child's life—grandparents, ex-partners, and caregivers—to help make messages as consistent as possible.

Throughout the book you'll also find the following tips and exercises will lay the groundwork for change in your household:

- *Tips.* Practical ideas for conveying your new expectations of your child

- *Parent Challenges* and *Self-Reflections*. Exercises and prompts to help you shift your own perspectives and parenting habits
- *Teachable Moments*. Ideas for leveraging events in your child's life into real learning opportunities
- *Consider This*. Facts, research, and other reminders that the stakes are high
- *Family Activities*. Fun and eye-opening activities that bring new ideas into your family culture
- *Keep Calm*. Words of wisdom at the end of each chapter to remind you you're not alone and how to stay the course when parenting feels like captaining a ship in a storm

You *can* do this: whatever your family situation, whatever your child's age, you can change your family dynamic and bring out the best in each of you.

Let's start with an informal evaluation. Take the following quiz to see where you and your child fall on the entitlement behavior continuum. By answering these questions honestly, you'll do yourself and your child a favor. Then read on for guidance on making gradual but consistent changes.

— QUIZ —

HOW ENTITLED IS MY CHILD?

Choose the answer that best reflects your family patterns.

1. When you tell your daughter no in public and she throws a temper tantrum:
   a. You ignore her behavior as best you can.
   b. Doesn't apply—you avoid going out in public with your daughter.
   c. You give in to quiet her down and avoid a scene.

2. When your son breaks the rules:
   a. You let him know that he did something wrong and use appropriate discipline.
   b. It depends on whether it was a big rule or a small one.
   c. You think he's just being a kid and let it go, since there will be plenty of time to correct habits later.

3. When it comes to your child's performance at school, you:
   a. Are proud if they try their best and work diligently.
   b. Expect them to be a high performer, and if not, you let them know they're not working hard enough.
   c. Are disappointed when they are just an average performer.

4. Your son's attitude toward possessions (toys when young, other items when older) is best reflected in the following statement:
   a. Takes care of possessions, both his and other people's, and expresses appreciation for what he has.
   b. Shows initial interest in new possessions, but the interest quickly fades and he then neglects them and requests something new.
   c. Is rarely satisfied with what he has, and constantly demands something newer, better, or what his friends have.

5. When considering habits of gratitude and respect, the following best reflects your child:

   a. Consistently says please and thank you—and means it—when interacting with others.

   b. Says please and thank you only after a reminder.

   c. Despite reminders, fails to express gratitude and respect when dealing with others.

6. When your daughter fails at something, you:

   a. Support her effort and use this experience as a way to improve future attempts.

   b. Tell her that failure is never acceptable and that she didn't work hard enough.

   c. Blame the failure on other factors or people and remind her that she is special and didn't deserve to fail.

7. When your son has trouble with a task, he often:

   a. Sticks with the task, occasionally asking for help but staying determined to see it through.

   b. Asks for help and then expects someone else to finish it for him.

   c. Walks away from the task, frustrated, with no desire to continue.

8. When you are speaking with another adult, your child will most likely:

   a. Wait for the adults to finish speaking before asking or saying anything.

   b. Interrupt the conversation, but remain quiet when told to wait for the conversation to end.

   c. Consistently interrupt and demand attention, often forcing you to end your conversation to attend to their needs or wants.

9. When your daughter has a disagreement with a friend, you typically:
    a. Discuss her feelings and thoughts about the situation, but allow her to work it through on her own.
    b. Intervene by contacting the parents of the other child to resolve the situation.
    c. Advise your daughter to end the friendship, because the friend doesn't appreciate how special she is.

10. When it comes to setting and enforcing limits, you are:
    a. Consistent
    b. Somewhat consistent
    c. Struggling with being consistent

Score your results:

1 point for each A   2 points for each B   3 points for each C

Total Score: _____

Interpret your score:

10: My family patterns are least likely to foster entitlement in my child.

11–14: My child has a slight degree of risk for entitled attitudes and behaviors.

15–20: My child has a moderate degree of entitlement risk.

21–30: My child is at high risk of feeling and acting entitled.

Entitlement
Is a
Family Dynamic

Part 1

1

What Is Entitlement?

Paul's sixteenth birthday was coming up, and he was excited. He wanted a new video game system as a birthday present, the powerful one that cost $500. When he asked his parents, they said, "Sorry, Paul. We can't afford that. Let's think about gifts closer to $100." Paul was angry. Many of his friends already had the new system, and he wanted one, too. "I'm turning sixteen! Doesn't that mean anything?" Paul said. "My game system is old. I can't play the new games." He yelled, "You're ruining my life!"

. . .

Do you feel like Paul's mom or dad? If so, know this: you have lots of company. At some point in the adventure of parenting, many of us realize that our kids are developing entitled attitudes. Your Paul—or Paula—might be three or eight, thirteen or eighteen. It might come as a shock to you, or as a gradually dawning realization, but you're seeing some behavior that, you must admit, seems spoiled. You're noticing an attitude: your child always seems to feel entitled to satisfy the wish or whim of the moment, whether it's a new game system, new clothes for a school dance, staying up late on a school night, or skipping a long-delayed chore in favor of a last-minute movie invitation.

Entitlement is a state of mind. People of all ages can have it. It's the assumption that the world owes us, that we deserve special privileges without having earned them. An entitled child assumes that top priority goes to *their* needs, *their* wants—like Paul, who ignores his parents' comment about what they can afford. But this assumption of priority doesn't hinge on how much money the family has, or doesn't have. The entitled child feels special, "just because I'm me."

Of course parents want to provide the best for their children. We want our children to be happy, healthy, and secure. Maybe we want our kids to feel unique, with a special place in the world; or we hope they can have all the things and opportunities we lacked in our own childhood. As we keep our kids' needs front and center, we may sacrifice our own well-being to make sure they never go without.

This is a recipe for entitlement.

If you see entitlement as only a problem for the affluent, think again. It's easy to picture the stereotypes: The parents who buy their sixteen-year-old a new car, then replace it when the door gets dented. The family whose extravagant birthday parties set a new standard every year. The parents who buy their teenager's way out of legal problems. Affluenza, as it's sometimes called, is the trait of wealthy kids who believe they deserve special treatment and dispensations because their family has money. And that definitely happens. But entitlement is more about the attitude than it is about material things, and that means it can occur in any income bracket.

Imagine the parents who are struggling to make ends meet: they might be overly permissive because they feel guilty that their daughter doesn't have all the stuff her classmates have—the clothes, the concert tickets, the sports gear. Or the mom who skips her doctor visit, jeopardizing her health so she can afford to buy her son the trendy jacket he wants. The divorced dad with partial custody who sets no rules when his eight-year-old visits, because a free-for-all is more fun. The mother in recovery who now overindulges her teenager, trying to compensate for her previous neglect. All of these scenarios can lead to feelings of entitlement, even when family income might be low.

All children make entitled statements from time to time. You might have heard your kid say things like this:

- "That's *my* truck—you can't have it!"
- "No, I won't make my bed. I don't feel like it."
- "I have to have that."
- "But I just emptied the dishwasher yesterday!"
- "I want that—buy it for me, Daddy!"

Parent Challenge: Together Time

Does your kid demand your attention all day long, whining when you're busy? Do they interrupt when you're talking to other adults? Do they expect you to drop everything when they "need" you? What your child is saying is, "I want you to think I'm important."

Try a new habit. Plan "together time"—at least ten to fifteen minutes a day when you give your child your undivided attention. Turn your phone off. Turn the television off. Play with him, read with her, ask questions about their interests. Then at some other time when your child is underfoot say, "How about you find something to do for now? We can talk (or play or go outside or read) later, during our together time." With this habit, you show your child they're important to you, but they're also developing skills to entertain themselves independently.

It's not a question of whether your kid will make demands— they will. It's how you respond to these demands that will shape your child, either toward an attitude of entitlement or toward a sense of responsibility and participation. Your child depends on you to be there for them and set limits in their life. They want to know that someone is in charge. They *need* someone to be in charge. It is the parent's job to say stop. Young children don't always understand that too much of a good thing can be bad. A child might see nothing wrong with eating five pieces of chocolate cake. As parents, we know that one piece of cake is enough. It's our job to say enough even when our child demands more.

Without limits, children believe they can have whatever they want, whenever they want it. Unless they learn otherwise, they believe they don't need to earn it, work for it, or give anything up to get it. They don't believe there should be any consequences for poor choices. And when there is a consequence, they often blame others rather than accepting blame themselves.

Will entitled children grow up to be narcissistic adults? That depends in part on what we mean by the term *narcissism*. Used casually, the word refers to self-absorbed behavior and perhaps an overinflated sense of self: these traits have a lot in common with entitled attitudes. But let's not confuse entitlement with narcissistic personality disorder (NPD), which is a mental illness. People with NPD most likely have a false sense of entitlement, but they also have other symptoms that push the problem into the range of a true mental disorder. These include expecting to be recognized as superior, assuming that only other people who are superior can relate to you, requiring constant admiration, taking advantage of others, and being unable to recognize the needs of others. Underlying these feelings of self-importance is usually a deep insecurity. Many people with NPD find it impossible to develop close relationships with others. Still, measures of narcissistic traits can shed light on personalities that are in the more normal range.

Today's young adults, especially those born in the late 1980s and 1990s, are sometimes called "Generation Me"—the entitled ones. But entitlement isn't a new phenomenon; it's just gaining ground. Jean Twenge makes that point in her book, *Generation Me: Why Today's Young Americans Are More Confident, Assertive, Entitled—and More Miserable Than Ever Before.* In the span of one generation—1982 to 2006—the proportion of students scoring above average on the Narcissistic Personality Inventory doubled, from about one-third to about two-thirds.[1] Narcissism and entitlement have been around as long as people have been around—some people will always act in self-centered ways—but today a false sense of entitlement is much more prevalent in our youth.

Children who are entitled are often unhappy, perhaps without knowing it. They probably don't enjoy the feeling of resilience, of knowing they can handle disappointments. If they've never had chores, they may not know the satisfaction of a job well done. Entitled kids often feel like something is missing. They're always looking to find happiness in the latest trend. They might have trouble making or keeping friends because of their neediness and constant demands. They are often seen as conceited and self-centered. They might need constant attention and reassurance that they are special.

And these attitudes don't magically disappear as children grow up. In chapter 4 we'll discuss the problems they might develop because of entitlement. For now, we'll simply say it can lead to laziness, lack of motivation, shaky problem-solving skills (and the escapist or addictive behavior that may accompany it), difficulties in relationships, and problems at school or work.

Sounds pretty bad, right?

Well, take a deep breath, and take heart. As discouraging as all of this sounds, you can turn the ship. Gradually and consistently, using this book, you can shift the patterns in your family—even if you fear they're pretty entrenched. Paul's parents are on the right track: they drew the line on the new video game system. (Let's just hope they don't waffle under pressure.) And with this book, you'll find that a less needy, more resilient home culture is actually a lot more fun—for everyone.

In the next several chapters of part 1, we'll explore how parental, societal, and cultural attitudes can either promote entitlement, or help correct or prevent it. And you'll learn some quick ways to apply those ideas now. In part 2, we'll turn to the more practical ways you can handle entitled attitudes in lots of everyday settings and situations.

Patterns of Entitlement: Some Red Flags

Kids with an attitude of entitlement are all about me and mine. They see the world through the what's-the-effect-on-me lens. This attitude usually comes across in children's daily behaviors. There are warning signs in kids' general behavior and in their interactions that may signal trouble. If the following behaviors seem very familiar to you, there's a good chance that entitled attitudes are alive and well in your child.

Warning Signs in Your Child's Behavior

- Your daughter seems driven by instant gratification and has trouble taking turns or waiting for a promised item. When she wants something, she wants it *now*.

- Your four-year old often demands a toy, candy, or other treat when you're in a store—and complains or cries until you give in.

- Nothing ever seems to satisfy your middle-schooler. If you buy them a game, they want another one. If you let them stay up half an hour later, they want an hour.

- After getting a desired gift for a birthday or holiday, your son is likely to tire of it quickly and want something else.

- Your teen can't separate wants from needs, and may use the reasoning that everyone else has one to explain what they want.

- Your child expects rewards for good behavior or good deeds.

Warning Signs in Your Child's Interactions

- Your son has learned to change his manner to get what he wants. If he thinks being sweet and helpful will help, he'll try that. If it doesn't work, he'll try a different approach.

- Your child hears your no as maybe, or later, and keeps pressing the issue.

- Your daughter doesn't show appreciation or gratitude for what she has or what people do for her.

- When your child gets in trouble at school, they expect you to talk to the teacher and get them out of trouble.

- Your son blames others when things go wrong and may have trouble apologizing.

- Your daughter rarely offers to help, and when she does, it's because there's something in it for her.

Of course, every child has some degree of entitlement: that's just part of being a child. Any child, on a bad day, can behave in these ways. But if you read these warning signs and repeatedly thought we were describing your child, then you have some work to do.

But hold on—there's more. We don't just see patterns of entitlement in our kids. We see them in ourselves, too. These next warning signs refer to *your* behavior. That's because these parental habits are a setup for entitled children. This is a family problem!

Warning Signs in Your Own Parenting Habits

- You often give your child a treat as an incentive to behave, or as a way to get them to stop misbehaving.

- You step in to solve problems with siblings or friends instead of letting them work it out on their own.

- Even when you say no to a request at first, you eventually cave in because you know your daughter will bug you until you do.

- You clean up after your son because it's easier than fighting with him to do it.

- You often end up completing chores or homework for your child because they have a hard time dealing with frustration.

Yes, you have your work cut out for you, and this book will help. Little by little, you can shift your family culture to nurture a more responsible, grateful child. Happy, healthy, and secure isn't enough. Let's aim for wise, too. Kids gain wisdom by opening their eyes to others' perspectives. Let's start with this simple family activity.

Family Activity: Pay It Forward

Start a weekly "pay it forward" challenge at home. At least once a week, each person needs to do something nice for someone—inside or outside the family. The catch is, it's done anonymously. There are plenty of things kids can do: shovel snow from a neighbor's sidewalk, leave a small anonymous gift for a friend, donate personal items to a local charity. This exercise is a healthy stretch for kids who are used to lots of praise and recognition. Keep a notebook so each person can write down the good deed. No one outside the family should see the notebook.

What Does an Entitlement-Free Kid Look Like?

Sometimes we don't know whether a certain habit is a problematic entitled behavior or just a phase a child is going through. So let's take a look at the big picture. If your child has most of the following qualities, their prospects for an entitlement-free adulthood are pretty good:

- *Has faith that the adults in their life will take care of their needs.* The child knows they can count on other people—such as parents, relatives, caregivers, teachers—and is confident that they will get what they need, even if it comes later.

- *Can delay gratification.* Imagine your child asks for a piece of cake an hour before supper. You might say, "Not now. You can have one after we eat." A non-entitled child might mope for a moment but will accept this answer. An entitled child might protest, "But I'm hungry now. I want a piece of cake right now!"

- *Has a sense that life is okay, even when it's disappointing or frustrating.* Non-entitled children have emotional resilience.

They can tolerate disappointment because they've heard the word no and take it seriously. They've learned to handle frustration because Dad stepped back and let them figure out how to solve a disagreement with a friend or a dispute with a coach. These kids develop faith in their own abilities; they know things will work out. But for entitled kids, emotional setbacks can feel more like the end of the world.

- *Has empathy for others.* Non-entitled children are learning to view situations from other kids' and adults' perspectives. Children who are entitled view the world and every interaction through the lens of "me." (What have you done for *me* lately?) They have trouble imagining how others feel.

- *Accepts limits set by others.* Suppose you're taking your child to the playground or your teen to the mall. Before leaving you say, "We need to make it quick this time. We'll stay for an hour, then meet up and come home." At the end of the hour, an entitled child at the playground might throw a tantrum or refuse to leave; the entitled teen might drag their feet. Non-entitled kids, even though they want to stay longer, will reluctantly accept and tolerate the limits.

- *Is thoughtful.* Children without a sense of entitlement find satisfaction in doing favors for other people without expecting anything in return. Their entitled peers usually do people favors only when there's something in it for them.

- *Is resourceful.* During times of frustration or disappointment, non-entitled kids might look for alternative solutions or find an acceptable replacement.

- *Can work through problems and find solutions.* Non-entitled children are able to work through age-appropriate problems to find a solution. Entitled kids expect others to fix their problems.

- *Understands the value of work and money.* Non-entitled kids learn the value of money and work by contributing to household tasks, taking part-time jobs (when old enough), and budgeting their money, starting with an allowance. Because many entitled children don't have to work or earn their belongings, they often continue to ask for more, without concern for how it's earned, or how plentiful or scarce it might be in their families.

- *Is appreciative and grateful.* Children who are non-entitled have a general sense of appreciation for both things and people. They thank people—and mean it—when given something, and accept limits to what they can have.

As you read this book and shift the patterns in your head and your household, you'll expect to see changes in your child. Be patient. It took years, in some cases many years, for your child to develop a sense of entitlement. It won't go away overnight. The older your child, the more they'll fight to keep life the same.

Do aim for consistency when you set new rules and limits: consistency is what gives them power. But don't expect perfection of yourself or your child. At times you will give in. At times you'll be too tired to fight the whining or tears. That's okay. We all give in at times, let a behavior slide, or lose our temper when our children don't treat us with respect. Take the advice that you'd give your child: Everyone makes mistakes. It's the effort that counts. Keep trying. Improve your consistency, and you will get there.

▼

KEEP CALM AND TOLERATE DISCOMFORT—
YOURS AND YOUR CHILD'S

Breaking patterns of entitlement can be tough. When your teen is outraged over your "unfair" new rules, or when you're tempted to cave in just to end your child's tantrum on the kitchen floor, remember this: *stay the course.* It will be uncomfortable for both you and your child, but you will both grow, know yourselves better, and find much greater happiness in the long run.

When you feel like you're in the trenches, keep these principles in mind:

- *It's okay if your child isn't happy at all times.* Sadness, disappointment, anger, and frustration are all normal, human emotions. The more you work to have your child avoid these emotions, the less prepared she will be when they inevitably show up in her life.

- *Natural consequences are often the best teacher.* Missing a class trip will help remind your child to hand in the permission slip. Dawdling to the dinner table might mean they miss their chance at the pot stickers or the eggrolls.

- *Your child notices what you tolerate as well as what you praise.* Kids know what behaviors they can get away with. If you praise respectful behavior, great. But if you also tolerate disrespectful or demanding behavior, it may continue. (An old saying puts it this way: to permit is to promote.)

- *There's no such thing as the perfect childhood.* Accept that your child's life will have ups and downs, triumphs and disappointments. Provide your child the consistency of your love.

2

"I Just Want Him to Be Happy"

HOW PARENTS ENABLE
ENTITLED ATTITUDES

Barb joined a local playgroup for her four-year-old, Taylor. On the first day, Barb sat off to the side with the other parents while Taylor joined the group of children on the floor. Taylor grabbed a toy from another boy's hands, saying, "I want to play with the car." Barb quickly intervened and gave the car back to the other child. But throughout the hour, Barb watched as Taylor steamrolled the other children—grabbing toys, insisting they play by his rules, then cutting into the line at snack time. When he didn't get his way in a group block-building project, he came over to Barb, crying. Barb was embarrassed. She mumbled some excuses to the other moms: "He's an only child and isn't always good at playing with others. I hope he'll get better at sharing and listening." Silently, though, Barb wondered: Did I do this? Did I create this selfish child?

• • •

The answer is yes. The buck always stops at the top, regardless of intent. Parenting plays a large role in whether children get along with others, whether they learn to share, and whether they grow up with entitled attitudes. As you'll see in chapter 3, social norms play a role, too, but parents must shoulder the bulk of the responsibility.

The good news is that you, as the parent, can reduce or eliminate your child's feelings of entitlement by changing how you act, react to the world around you, and interact with your child.

Entitlement at Home

Like most parents, Barb didn't start out by deciding she was going to spoil her child. More likely, Barb just wanted to provide the best of everything to Taylor. She wanted him to be happy and was willing to go to great lengths to make sure he felt he was special, including letting him have his way at home and giving him plenty of toys. Barb's attitude that Taylor should never want for anything contributed to his sense of entitlement. It's a common myth that a parent's job is to prevent pain, sadness, and frustration. Instead, parents should focus on helping children learn to *tolerate and deal with unpleasant feelings*. Disappointments are an inevitable part of life. Bouncing back from them is an essential life skill.

Remember, entitlement comes from an attitude, not from money or things. It occurs in homes where there isn't enough money to pay the bills and in homes where money flows

---

Tip: Parents, Get on the Same Page

Avoid sending your child mixed messages. When two parents are involved, they need to work together. If they disagree on parenting methods or if their judgment frequently differs, it might help to seek parental coaching, talk with a family therapist, or attend parenting classes together.

---

freely. Some parental assumptions contribute to a sense of entitlement:

- My child is special and unique.
- My daughter deserves the best of everything.
- Sacrificing my needs so I can give my son what he wants is part of parenting.
- I want my child to be my friend.
- I want my child to always like me.

Unfortunately, these beliefs work to satisfy a parent's ego rather than working toward creating a responsible child.

There's no doubt that a smile on a child's face brings absolute joy to parents. But let's remember that, for all of us, real and sustaining happiness comes from within. The happiness that comes from possessions, strokes, admiration, and other external rewards is fleeting in comparison. Our job as parents is to build the inner resilience that makes for lifelong satisfaction. Consider the following two scenarios.

Sandy and her daughter, Ava, went shopping for a dress for senior prom. When they reached the mall, Ava passed by several shops that had prom dresses, saying, "Everyone will be wearing those dresses—I want something unique." She headed to a bridal shop. After trying on ten dresses, she chose one in a princess style with a full skirt. Ava fully expected to walk into the prom and have everyone tell her how beautiful she looked—she even hoped for a little envy. Although the $500 price tag put her over budget, Sandy paid for it. Senior prom is once in a lifetime, she thought. Ava deserves to have a special night. Afterward, they went out for dinner to celebrate. On prom night, Sandy chaperoned, beaming because her daughter had the most beautiful dress at the prom.

Carmen was also planning for her senior prom, saving money from her part-time job for several months to buy a dress. She asked her mother, Bianca, to come shopping with her. At the mall they checked out discount stores and looked for dresses under $100. Carmen tried on several, coming out of the dressing room to show Bianca each time. After checking several stores, they found a dress that looked great on Carmen and was well within her budget. Afterward, they stopped for ice cream. On prom night, Carmen looked wonderful and had a great sense of pride that she'd bought the dress with her own money. When the pictures arrived, Bianca proudly displayed Carmen's prom picture.

A sense of entitlement often begins early in life when parents don't instill a sense of responsibility and gratefulness. In the previous example, Ava believed she deserved an expensive bridal-shop dress, even though her mother couldn't really afford it. All her life, Ava had been told how special she is, how she deserves the best of everything. Ava relied on her mother to take care of all her needs. She wasn't grateful for the dress—she expected it. She derived her sense of happiness from external sources: the dress, the admiration, the envious looks.

Carmen, on the other hand, worked weekends at a part-time job, saving from her paycheck to buy a dress. All her life, Carmen had been taught that hard work and responsibility were important. She didn't expect a new dress but was thrilled and grateful that she could buy it. Carmen found her happiness in her internal feelings of self-worth.

Children may develop a sense of entitlement if any or all of following are true:

- They have few chores or responsibilities at home.
- Few rules govern their behavior.

- Their parents allow them to set their own schedule.
- Others shower them with material things.
- They are lavished with their parents' time and attention.

When children are brought up in this type of environment, they end up viewing the world from an I-am-therefore-I-deserve perspective. They believe their purpose in life is to have fun and be happy. They don't know how to handle disappointment and expect someone to rescue them from mishaps or difficult situations.

The Rise of the "Kids-First" Family System

The idea of unearned privilege has deep roots in human society. In many cultures, children born into royalty or nobility were given riches and titles—literal "entitlement"—simply because it was their birthright. These children might grow up believing they deserved more than those they ruled. So historically, entitlement has often rightfully been associated with the rich and powerful.

But in the United States today, it's rampant in every socio-economic class. The youth of today are often called "the entitlement generation." Many people believe that those born in the 1980s and early 1990s, often called *millennials*, feel more entitled than previous generations. While this might be true, it is important to remember that this phenomenon has been around for many years and can show up no matter when you or your child were born.

Still, the last four decades have seen a dramatic shift. In the 1970s many child psychology experts decided that we faced a self-esteem crisis. They believed that lifting children up, praising them, and focusing only on the positive was the remedy for what ails society, with its crime and injustice; that it would promote a stronger sense of self and self-worth. The self-esteem movement was born. In the next several decades, *praise* became the watchword. Parents were told to tell their children they were special and unique, that any negative feedback could damage their children's self-esteem. They were told the best way to make their children feel good about themself was to always be positive.

Parents, and society in general, took this to heart. Previously many parents, teachers, and coaches had habitually withheld praise, saying, "You did okay, but you can do better" because they feared the child would "get a big head." But this new theory said that philosophy was damaging children. It said we were raising children who didn't want to try because no matter how hard they tried it wasn't good enough. And the new theory stuck for quite a while.

But now the self-esteem explosion of the 1970s, '80s, and '90s seems to have backfired. A study published in 2015 found that children who were told by parents that they were special or superior became more narcissistic as they grew up. These children developed an overinflated sense of self, were fixated on material things, and showed a lack of empathy toward others.[2] Of course we all have a need to be admired by others. But what seems to be missing in these generations is a sense of balance. It's true that children (and adults) need validation, but they also need to learn responsibility and how to tolerate loss. The problem with the self-esteem movement was that it lacked balance. It focused too much on praise and gratification, and not enough on responsibility and skills for independence.

In addition to overindulging children emotionally and materially, our culture has seen a dramatic shift from community to individual over the past century. As people became more mobile, neighborhood communities started disappearing. Today, many people say they either don't know their neighbors or know them only well enough to wave hello. In the past, this would have been unthinkable. In many places, neighbors were like an extended family. Children played outdoors together; parents kept an eye on other people's kids; families gathered together for street parties, picnics, and other celebrations.

And among families, the shift is even more dramatic. Children move across the country instead of across town. Siblings and cousins see each other only at weddings and funerals. The family unit has become disjointed. The result is nothing less than a psychic shift in identity: now more than ever, Americans see themselves as individuals rather than communities, which in turn leads to a looking-out-for-number-one mentality. After all, if you don't know your relatives, your neighbors, or others within your community, you don't need to consider their needs. You are the only one who matters.

An Entitlement-Promoting Society

It's a fast-paced world out there. The U.S. economy is such that many families rely on two incomes. With instant communication, our jobs often sneak into our home life. The workplace is competitive and so is higher education. For children, school has become more demanding, even beginning in kindergarten. In our Western culture we have been taught to never be satisfied, to always strive for more and better. We want a better car, a bigger house, more clothes, and the newest phone or tablet. Parents have to work longer and harder just to keep up. Even the most well-intentioned parents feel the pull to give, give, give—so they, and their children, won't slide back. We live by the motto "Good, better, best. Never let it rest." The problem is, *best* does not exist. It is a perfectionist ideal. We therefore live in an endless cycle of never being satisfied.

The pace of the world today has changed us, and not always for the better:

- With instantaneous texting, emails, instant messaging, and social media, children expect other parts of their life will be just as immediate. They have trouble delaying gratification and waiting for a result or a reward.

- Parents want to give their child every advantage in a competitive society, so they buy them the latest device to give them an edge. Now we see three-year-olds playing alone on a tablet instead of playing outdoors with other children.

- With busy schedules, children have fewer responsibilities at home than in previous generations. Parents don't always have the time or patience to teach their child how to, say, clean the oven or mow the lawn. It's often easier for parents to do it themselves.

- Parents might feel guilty because work schedules limit the time they spend with children, so they indulge them in other ways: bending the rules, exempting them from chores, giving gifts.

- With higher stress levels from balancing work and home, parents might find it easier to give in to a child "just this once" rather than stand their ground. But just this once easily turns into every time.

- Children's screen time increases because televisions, computers, tablets, and phones keep them occupied and give parents a chance to do chores or unwind.

Teachable Moment: How Much Is It Worth?

When saying no to your child, think about the lesson you want them to learn. Imagine your pre-teen asks you to buy a video game for them. Instead of simply refusing, provide them with a lesson about the value of money. Ask them the price, tell them about minimum wage, then have them determine how many hours they'd need to work to earn enough money to buy the game (you can introduce taxes as well). If it's not a hardship and you believe your teen deserves it, you could offer a number of hours of extra household work—tasks beyond their regular chores—in exchange for the game.

On top of this accelerating pace, many parents have become lax in their expectations of their children. Many don't expect teens to work while going to school because they don't want to overburden them. Instead, they give their teens money whenever they want something. Teens don't learn the value of earning what they own and therefore don't feel the pride of ownership.

Bradley's high-school friends had all gotten the newest smartphone, but Bradley had last year's model. When he asked his parents to buy him the latest model, they agreed, not wanting Bradley to suffer disappointment or feel inferior to his friends. They bought him the phone. But within weeks, the screen was cracked. When Bradley asked for another one, he didn't take any responsibility or even apologize. "These things happen," he said. This time his parents didn't relent. They told him he'd have to earn the money himself: he could do extra household tasks for pay, and they insisted he find a part-time job, too. At first Bradley was angry. But as he started making money, his attitude changed. He made enough to buy the new phone, and this time, since he'd paid for it, he also bought a case and was much more careful with it.

Another way parents encourage entitled behavior is by trying to fix problems for their children. Life is not always easy. It's filled with ups and downs, disappointments and triumphs. And it's through the challenges of life that we learn about our inner strengths. We learn we can make it through even the most difficult times. As parents, it pains us to see our child sad, hurt, or upset. We want to fix it right away. But when we shield our children from negative emotions, we take away their chance to learn about themselves.

> Ten-year-old Rachel had a fight with her best friend, Mai. She came home from school upset about Mai's nasty comment to her—so upset she couldn't eat dinner that night. Rachel's mother called Mai's mother right after dinner to find out what happened and to insist that Mai apologize. Mai's mom became defensive and blamed Rachel for the argument. Neither mother gave the girls a chance to sort out their differences on their own.

Calling the teacher to complain about a bad grade, interfering in childhood squabbles, buying a treat to soothe a disappointment, excusing children from chores because they're upset, or immediately blaming someone else for a problem: all of these parental reactions deprive kids of developing resilience. By stepping in, we're often sending the message that we don't have faith in their ability to work through a challenge. Yes, it's important for us to be there, to offer emotional support and let our child know we believe in them. But solving their problems for them? That only hurts them in the long term.

Your Child Is Not Your "Friend"

A parent's role is both functional and emotional. You are there to take care of your child's needs. In infancy, the functional part is evident: changing diapers, feeding, providing clothes. You take care of the emotional part by holding, singing to, and talking to your baby. But as your child grows, these roles are less defined. If we want our children to have successful, independent lives, they need to develop resilience early in life. You want your child to see you as someone they can talk to about problems, but you also want your child to become more independent. We don't want them to rely on us to solve their problems. In many ways, parenting is a one-sided relationship. Your child can come to you with problems, but you can't go to them with yours. You're more like a coach, in fact. In a parent-child relationship someone needs to be in charge and that is you. We'll discuss this further in chapter 6, "Respect: Modeling It, Teaching It."

Tip: Let Kids Be Kids

We need to be careful to treat our kids as kids, not miniature adults. The fact that our children or teens may act mature does not mean they are capable of handling sensitive information with adult judgment. Many well-intentioned parents make this mistake. Use your own judgment and avoid burdening your kid with too much information.

Three Ways to Start Making Changes

Later, in part 2 of this book, you'll learn practical steps for "un-entitling" your child in a variety of ways. But for now, let's look at three ways you can start shifting your family culture: using praise wisely, sharing household responsibilities, and practicing gratitude.

Praise: Use It Wisely

You are right. Your child is special and unique. They have talents and strengths. They are wonderful. All of this is true . . . to a point. Telling your five-year-old son he's the best artist in the world when he brings you a drawing isn't helpful. Telling your ten-year-old daughter she's the best soccer goalie you ever saw isn't helpful either. These types of statements give your child an overinflated sense of self. Your daughter might protest when her coach decides to have her sit on the bench so a teammate can take a turn. Your son might not understand why nobody else is oohing and aahing over his artwork. Overpraising children gives them a distorted view of their abilities. For praise to be meaningful, it needs to be true and realistic. These tips can help:

- *Make it specific.* Positive feedback helps children further develop their skills. "I like how you blended the colors in this picture." "You did a good job pitching today. I saw you were focused, and you threw more accurately than you did in the last game." This type of praise gives your child specific feedback they can use to continue to improve.

- *Praise effort over talent.* When you praise talent, you tell your child they don't need to work hard—they can just rely on their gift. That's the unspoken message behind labels such as "the best artist" or "the best goalie." Praise is more effective when you praise effort. "You played that piano piece very expressively. I can tell you really practiced that fast section this week."

- *Notice and praise your child's willingness to rise to a challenge.* Point out that trying is worthwhile, even when the goal seems difficult. In fact, being willing to try is more important than the outcome. In other words, you don't need to praise the A on a test, but you want to actively support the *effort* that went into the A—or the B or even the C—if it was an extra-tough challenge for your child.

- *Praise more than one aspect of life.* Balance the praise you give your child by recognizing efforts in different areas of their life: educational, social, spiritual, and emotional. Praise, when given correctly, helps your child grow. If you reserve it for only one area of your child's life, you are not supporting growth in the other areas.

- *Praise the ability to adapt.* Throughout your child's life, they will receive criticism and feedback; how they handle these can have major consequences. Praise the ability to take criticism and feedback and make changes accordingly. This often gets missed, but is a wonderful skill for kids to develop.

- *Be truthful.* Your child can tell if you are handing out empty praise, and it often confuses them. They probably know that whatever they did isn't that great. But if you say it is, they learn they can get away with less than their best effort. If you want to praise a less than stellar effort, find something to be positive about without praising the overall result. "Nice work on those graphs for your science project." This way your praise is still honest.

- *Use the quality over quantity rule.* You don't need to offer praise for every little thing. Praise used selectively and sincerely has more of an impact.

Chores: The Gift of Responsibility

How does your child help around your home? Are they expected to put away their toys? Straighten their room? Take dinner dishes to the sink? For many harried parents, it's easier and quicker to simply do these tasks instead of insisting their child do so. But chores, starting from a young age, are what teach your child a sense of responsibility and accomplishment. Chores also give children a sense of belonging, pride, and ownership of the family and home. It teaches them that families work best when everyone helps. These tips will help:

- *Make chores age-appropriate.* A two-year-old can help pick up toys before going to bed. A three-year-old can carry silverware or napkins to the dinner table. Elementary-age children can fold clothes and straighten up a room. By middle school most children can do a load of wash, vacuum, clean the dishes, or even cook a meal. By the teen years, your children should be able to do most household tasks, including mopping floors, cleaning the bathroom, mowing the lawn, and watching over younger children.

- *Be specific with expectations.* "Clean your room" is not a clear direction. "Make your bed, hang up your clothes, and vacuum the rug" is much clearer. Your child can't live up to expectations unless they know what they are. Be as specific as possible.

- *Be consistent.* If you are inconsistent about having your child complete their chores, you're setting yourself up for constant arguments. Whether chores are daily, weekly, or both, set a time when chores should be finished, then follow up to make sure they are.

- *Don't insist on perfection.* Look for effort rather than focusing on the outcome. If your child tries but doesn't get the chore done perfectly, praise the effort.

- *Don't jump in to finish.* It's tempting to jump in to finish a task that is taking too long or not getting done properly, but your child will have a better sense of accomplishment if you let them finish to the best of their ability.

- *Foster an attitude of working toward common goals.* Chores, or household tasks, are part of maintaining a household, and every family member should participate. These help children feel part of something bigger than themselves. (In chapter 10, "Kids, Chores, and Money," we'll discuss linking tasks to allowances. That's an option, although some parenting experts question it.)

Appreciate: Practice Gratitude

One of the hallmarks of entitlement is expecting rather than appreciating. But actively practicing gratitude is one of the keys to general happiness and success in life. How do we teach our children to be grateful for what they have, rather than always focusing on what they don't have? Gratitude is a muscle—use it! The best way is to practice gratitude yourself every day:

- *Add words of gratitude to your everyday speech.* There are many ways to show gratitude, with or without the word *thanks.* "Aren't fresh apples delicious at this time of year?" "What a beautiful sunset—thanks for telling me to look out the window!" "It is nice to spend time together." By pointing out things that make you happy, you are showing gratitude.

- *Start a simple gratitude ritual.* Many families take time at the dinner table to share one thing they are thankful for—or perhaps one good thing that happened that day—letting each person take a turn. You can also help your child start and maintain a gratitude journal.

- *Say thank you.* Send thank-you notes for gifts; thank people for favors they do for you. Thank the cashier in the store, the bus driver, the person who serviced your car. Show your appreciation as often as possible.

- *Give to others.* You can volunteer as a family, donate clothes and toys to a local shelter, or buy holiday gifts for a less fortunate family. Or it can be spontaneous: help a neighbor carry groceries, bring dinner to a friend who is ill or elderly, or stop on the street to pick up and return a dropped glove. When you give to others, in ways large or small, you show your child that other people are important. Point out that some people have more, some people have less, but we can all be grateful and happy for what we have.

- *Look for the positive.* Bad things happen but that doesn't mean you can't look at them with a positive spin. Adopt the attitude that the glass is half full. When your teen comes home disappointed that they didn't win the election for class president, point out what they gained from the campaign: some new friends, a better understanding of how campaigns and government work, and lessons on marketing.

Change Starts with You

Parents are powerful models. Yes, we can gradually change our children's sense of entitlement to one of appreciation and responsibility. But we must first change ourselves. It's up to parents to learn to say no, to teach accountability, to practice empathy and gratefulness, and to distinguish wants from needs. Most importantly, it's up to parents to instill a sense of independence and resilience in our children.

Raising a confident and responsible child starts with you. Your child learns from your actions, even more than from your words. How do you treat others? Do you tend to blame others, or do you look for your own responsibility in the matter? Do you actively practice gratitude? Before you can change your child's behaviors, you need to look at your own. Do you act entitled? If so, the first step is to adjust your own behaviors.

Change starts with you.

KEEP CALM AND BE THE ADULT IN THE ROOM

Every child is an individual. But does your child also mirror you? Let your child's behavior provide insight into your own. If you don't like everything you see in that mirror, forgive yourself. And then look ahead. For parents, true behavior change involves soul searching, acceptance, and taking responsibility for what may have been missteps on your part. Just as your child might buck your attempts at changing your family dynamics, you might unintentionally buck the need to make changes within yourself. It might feel overwhelming. Start small. One small change, consistently observed, might lead to a bigger change.

Choose one or two parenting habits to work on first. Trying to change everything at once is overwhelming and rarely works. You might choose from the three habits outlined in this book:

- *Practice giving balanced praise.* Rather than automatically applauding what your child does, think first. What is genuinely praiseworthy? Praise that specifically. Selective, sincere praise has a bigger impact.

- *Ask your child to help with a task:* "Could you please put one napkin next to each plate at the table?" These small,

— *continued* —

specific requests can lay the groundwork for a more systematic sharing of household chores.

- *Start a gratitude journal.* The best way to teach a child to be grateful is to practice it yourself. Every evening for thirty days, write down five things you are thankful for.

3

The Entitlement Culture

Yes, entitlement starts at home with family patterns. But as children grow and step out into the world, budding me-first attitudes can find a lot of support. Let's take a look at how entitled attitudes show up at school and in sports and other activities, and how it's fed by advertising, social media, and other cultural influences in our kids' daily lives.

Looking Out for Number One: The Rise of Individualism

For most of human history, people have banded together, finding safety and efficiency in group living. Multiple people could more easily fend off dangers: human attackers, animals, natural disasters. Staying in groups gave everyone a better chance of survival.

It also made sense socially. Each person was part of a family, which was part of a clan or neighborhood, which was part of a tribe or community, and so on. Each person belonged; each contributed their own skills to the group. We were protected physically, economically, and emotionally through the various groups we belonged to. In the early United States, agrarian and small-town life sustained these traditions in large part.

But in today's largely urban and suburban society—and in many rural areas, too—these groups have changed dramatically.

Families are smaller; extended families are scattered. Neighbors barely know one another. Communities struggle to find people willing to be leaders. We've become a society of individuals rather than a communal society. Our focus has shifted from civic responsibility to self-gratification, from meaningful contributions to personal success.

This change actually began more than a century ago, with the broad-based shift from agriculture and manual labor to more skilled labor and office work. More people went on to higher education and had greater wealth, which promoted individualism, according to a study published in 2015.[3]

Single-person households offer one measure of the trend. More people are single than in the past. The percentage of adults in the United States who live alone has grown fivefold in the last century, from 5 percent in the 1920s to about 27 percent in 2013.[4] Some theorize this is a result of the high divorce rate, but studies also show that Americans prefer privacy and, when finances allow, they often choose to live alone.

Has our sense of entitlement grown in lockstep with the rise of individualism? Where once we relied on a group to keep us safe, is a sense of entitlement a natural outcome as we prioritize individual needs over the collective good?

Me-First at School

Attitudes of entitlement are found even in the youngest elementary school children. Paula Gardner, a school psychologist for the Southern Columbia Area School District in Pennsylvania, says that many children enter school believing they don't need to follow rules. Some don't have a respect for authority, talking to teachers as if they were equals. Many find it difficult, if not impossible, to take responsibility for their actions.[5]

In Gardner's school district, teachers and school administrators are trying to curtail the effects of entitlement. They created school-wide behavioral programs that focus on being respectful, completing work, and resolving conflicts. But Gardner says those efforts are sometimes undermined by parents, ironically enough. Too often, when a child does misbehave, he goes home and tells a story that isn't true, blaming classmates or even teachers for the problem. Some parents then march into school complaining about their child's treatment, and when they don't get the answer they want, they move up the hierarchy, from teacher to principal to superintendent, sometimes all the way to the school board. When parents find it hard to accept that their child misbehaves, it often limits what a school can do. Discipline methods might depend on the parents' likely resistance, rather than on consistent, fair application of the rules.

> Fourth-grader Manuel was smart but often disrupted the class, interrupting the teacher, Mrs. Collins, and using inappropriate language. Mrs. Collins had repeatedly talked to him about his behavior, to no avail. Then she brought it up in a meeting with Manuel's mother, who insisted Mrs. Collins was being too hard on him. Finally she gave Manuel an after-school detention for the next Thursday, and his parents were notified to pick him up afterward. But when school let out on Thursday, Manuel's mom showed up at the school office, insisting that he be allowed to leave. Because a school cannot keep a child against a parent's will, Manuel went home with his mom, circumventing the detention for his disruptive behavior.

Some schools want to bridge the gap between teacher and student, hoping to make students feel more comfortable coming to teachers with questions. Students are allowed and possibly encouraged to call teachers by first name. Administrators in these schools believe that the casual relationship will be more conducive to open learning and exploration of topics. But it also has the potential to blur lines between students and authority figures. Students might feel more apt to question rules or disregard teachers' knowledge and experience. What message does this send to children who must later enter the workplace? Will they have a sense that they're on equal terms with their supervisor? Will they believe they can undermine, ignore, or challenge any authority figure?

Meanwhile, this attitude extends to college. Professors note that many students believe their grades should be based on effort rather than the content of papers and tests. A student might say, "But I worked hard on this paper, I should have at least gotten a B" or "I showed up for class every day—that should count as part of my grade." A study completed in 2008 found that almost 67 percent of college students felt that trying hard should result in a good grade; about 40 percent thought that completing most of the required reading should give them at least a B. But maybe the most disturbing statistic was that more than 16 percent thought that professors should let them answer their mobile phones during class, a clear indication of a false sense of entitlement: "I should be allowed to do what I want, when I want it, without regard to others."[6]

With the rise of the Internet in the past few decades, general attitudes toward education have shifted, too. With easy access to all the information you could possibly need, students—and some parents—do not place the same value on education they once did. Why study for social studies or science when you can find an answer to any question within a few seconds? Society is now designed around a system of information access rather than earned or learned knowledge—let alone the sheer love of learning.

Me-First in Sports and Other Activities

Any given Saturday during the spring and fall months, America's towns and cities are filled with basketball games, and its parks and ball fields are filled with kids playing baseball, football, soccer, and other sports. If you stand on the sidelines, you will hear parents and coaches telling the players how great they are, even when they aren't. Not all children are meant to play competitive sports. But that doesn't mean we shouldn't give them a chance to try and encourage their efforts. Still, it probably doesn't give Jacob or Jane a correct sense of self if we tell them their baseball skills are "the best" when they can't throw a ball more than ten feet. It might be better to explain that baseball might not be the best fit, but there are plenty of other sports and activities in the world to try. Guiding children toward the right activity to match their skills and interests will boost their long-term self-esteem more than giving them false praise to make them feel good in the moment.

Teachable Moment: When the Kid's Not a Natural

When your child signs up for an activity and it turns out it isn't a good fit, it may be a perfect opportunity to talk about handling awkward feelings or critical feedback from teachers or coaches. Rather than praising your child for something they obviously aren't good at, discuss what went well and what didn't. Talk about the choice to use the feedback to improve their skills or decide to change focus to a different area. It's fine to experiment and change course.

Participant Trophies: A Boost or a Bust?

Traditionally, trophies are given only to winners and other high performers: they are earned, whether in sports, academic competitions, or other settings. But in recent decades—since the self-esteem boom of the 1970s—the practice of giving "participant trophies" has become widespread in elementary, middle, and high schools. Such trophies are meant to lift kids up, make them feel good about being part of a team, and encourage them to continue to try. Parents and coaches who advocate for giving every child on the team a trophy at the end of the season believe that each child's effort should be rewarded. Not every child is a natural athlete, they say, but all of them should be recognized for trying.

Not everyone thinks that way. Many say that participant trophies are a form of over-praise, part of the unrelenting culture of strokes and gratification that is hurting our children in the long run. Participation, they say, is voluntary and should be its own reward. Children shouldn't be honored just for showing up. Others argue that we aren't actually honoring children for showing up, we are honoring their parents for signing the child up and paying the fee. They believe that participant trophies are simply what the parents "bought" when they paid the registration fee.

And what about those children who actually deserve a special pat on the back? The ones who came in first or excelled at teamwork? Aren't they being cheated of a merit-based reward? When participant trophies are given to all children, it devalues all of the trophies. Imagine that your son, a Little League pitcher, had more strikeouts than anyone else in the league this season. The coach gives him his trophy and recognizes his achievement, then says, "But everyone here is an MVP. Everyone on the team is important." The coach doesn't want the other children to feel bad, but in doing so, he minimizes the achievement of the young pitcher. To quote from the movie *The Incredibles*, "When everyone's super, no one will be."

In fact, NFL linebacker James Harrison wouldn't let his two sons accept such trophies. In 2015, he posted a picture of the trophies they received for participation with the caption, "These trophies will be given back until they EARN a real trophy . . . sometimes your best is not enough, and that should drive you to want to do better."[7]

Critics also say that even if coaches want to recognize effort over excellence, participant trophies miss the mark because everyone gets one—not only the kid who worked hard at every single practice but still didn't excel, but also the kid who missed many practices and didn't try very hard. If a coach believes a special effort should be recognized, rather than give everyone a trophy, a better way might be to give small, meaningful awards for effort, perseverance, or sportsmanship to those who deserve them.

> Seven-year-old Damien was a beginner in Little League baseball. He loved the game but was having a hard time catching the ball. So he worked on it. At practice he asked his coach to throw him the ball; at home he asked his mom or dad to throw it. When no one was around, he tossed the ball in the air and tried to catch it. All his effort paid off when, during a game one glorious day, he held up his mitt in the outfield and caught a fly ball. The crowd went wild (at least his parents did), hollering, "Yeah, Damien! Woo-hoo!" On the way home, his parents praised Damien for his real accomplishment—having the inner strength to accept the challenge of improving and to practice every day. They helped

> him see that the real reward wasn't the cheering crowd, but his feelings of bliss and accomplishment for having worked so hard he *could* catch the ball. In other words, they helped him learn the difference between praise and reward.

It could also be argued that for some kids, participant trophies lessen the motivation to improve. If your daughter sees her friend, teammate, or leaguemate receiving a first-place trophy, she might want one, too. Next season she might push herself harder so she also can have a trophy. But when everyone gets a trophy, what's her reason to look for ways to improve? She'll get a trophy anyway.

"You Deserve It!" . . . Resisting Consumerism

We live in a consumer-driven society. We're urged to work hard so we can chase the American dream, seeing material things as the way to happiness. There is an incessant pressure for us to buy more and better things. We want a bigger house, a faster car. Our children see this, and they want to join in the pursuit of things. They want the latest electronics because their friends have them. They want clothes from whatever store is trendy this year. All around us companies are vying for our money and our attention.

The average American child is exposed to about 40,000 television commercial messages per year. Advertisers spend about $17 billion annually trying to influence our children's thinking.[8] Commercials tend to blur the lines between wants and needs. They place products—or services, or experiences—in front of our children with the underlying message that these will make them happier, smarter, cooler, more popular. Young children, particularly, don't have the cognitive skills or perspective to look critically at these ads. They see something fun or attractive—from breakfast cereals to skateboards—and they believe they need it.

We want it! We deserve it! A McDonald's ad in the 1980s told us, "You deserve a break today." In 2008, a Chase credit card commercial used the lyrics "I want it all, and I want it now," from a song by Queen, to promote charging purchases even if we couldn't afford them. A classic commercial from L'Oreal ended with "because you're worth it." We hear those words from commercials, from friends, from relatives, and from our own family. And hey, in some ways they might be true. We work hard; we sacrifice our wants to cover our needs. We might deserve a break today, but that might mean a nap or a walk outside. Instead, our consumer culture tells us to spend money on that break: an expensive piece of athletic gear, a spa visit, a mountain bike. (And if we're enjoying a break today, let's not confuse today with every day.)

It's no wonder our children have entitled attitudes. On their screens, on the airwaves, even in their own home, they are

---

Parent Challenge: Introduce the "Earn It" Idea

What's the difference between deserving and earning something? Imagine you're planning a vacation. For several months you've been putting away a portion of your paycheck to pay for it. If the job's been busy, you might say you "deserve" the break, but in reality, you have earned the vacation. You work every day, you've earned time off, you've saved money, and now you choose to spend it on a vacation. You don't *deserve* the vacation: that implies that someone else needs to give it to you. You have *earned* it. Try using that phrase—*earn it*—when talking with your child. Send the message that we must earn what we want.

---

being told they *deserve* something that costs money. The difference is that when we, as adults, pay for that treat—for ourselves or for our children—we have earned the money to do so. We have gotten up each morning and gone to work. We've earned the right to determine how to spend it. Our children are bombarded with messages such as *you need* and *you deserve*, but the truth is they really don't either need or deserve most of the products being advertised.

Parents can help children, even young ones, sort through advertising messages by discussing the differences between wants and needs. Other lessons help children understand how to live within their budget and keep their long-term goals in mind. For example, a family vacation can give parents and their child quality time together, which is always good. But if spending money on a vacation means you will have to sacrifice later, you need to decide which is more important.

Teachable Moment: Need It or Want It?

Keep a large chart in your kitchen with two columns labeled *Needs* and *Wants.* Every time your child asks you for something, have them figure out which column it belongs in and write it there. (A younger child can draw a picture of the item, or find a picture to paste on the chart.) If it's a want, explain the options. Can your family buy it either now or later, after all needs are taken care of? Or is the budget too tight? Are there other wants that are higher on the list for the family's well-being? Could your child earn the money to pay for this want? How?

Parent Challenge: Teach Needs vs. Wants

Understanding the difference between needs and wants—and applying that understanding in everyday situations—is a life skill that will serve your child well. It's not always easy, because wants and needs vary in different situations, and there are plenty of gray areas. So consider this a thought exercise—one that offers you and your kid a reference point for many future conversations.

Basic personal needs include:

- *Food.* Three healthy meals a day are a need.
  (Wants include snacks, specialty foods, soda, or candy. Help your child see the difference.)

- *Shelter,* including basic utilities.
  (Phone and Internet-related services may be a gray area between needs and wants, depending on employment, school policies, and so on.)

- *Clothing.* Basic clothes and shoes are a need.
  (Special items such as designer jeans and high-tech sneakers are wants; so are accessories and jewelry.)

- *Health care,* including basic health and hygiene products, is a need.

Family needs include:

- *Transportation.* Car and/or public transit expenses are often a large budget item, and most families need transportation for employment. (Vacation-related travel, however, is a want.)

- *Insurance.* Health care and other policies provide a family safety net.

- *Home maintenance and furnishings.* Needs include a bed to sleep in and basic maintenance that ensures the home is safe.

continued

---

continued

- *Home technology* at some level is often considered
a need today, especially for job-related communications
—but this is certainly a gray area.
- *Other work- or school-related needs.* Uniforms or
other appropriate clothing are a need, as are work
tools and school supplies.

On top of these broad categories, you might have a few
other true needs specific to your family. But strictly speaking,
everything else is a want.

In chapter 10, "Kids, Chores, and Money," we'll go beyond
needs and wants to two more categories: savings and gifts for
others. But for now, keep it simple—use practice and repetition
to help children make the all-important distinction between
needs and wants.

The Internet: A Ready-Made
and Dangerous Entitlement Bubble

The Internet is indeed an amazing tool, and many of us today
are digital natives because of it. But digital culture has increas-
ingly enabled a me-centric worldview for kids by creating a
bubble that is easy for them to step into, sometimes before
parents even realize it has happened. By the time parents do,
kids might already have absorbed that living in this bubble of
ever-available information is normal—the information is right
at their fingertips, so they must be entitled to it. It's an easy
leap from that to questioning why they have to, for instance,
do their math longhand when they could google it or use a
calculator instead.

This online entitlement culture is dangerous, not only because it feeds our kids, but because our kids feed it in return. In the bubble, excessive shopping, digital piracy, and online bullying are normal. Marketers have profiled us, showing us the products we're most likely to buy, hoping to trigger the I-want-that! response in all of us. We can access a huge selection of music, movies, television shows, and books online for free. Since it's all there for the taking, many feel entitled to take it, even when downloading it is illegal. The everyone-does-it mentality is even more dangerous when it comes to online bullying, because the peer pressure to participate is very strong and the damage caused so profound. Whether it's shopping, stealing music, or bullying, the more your child and their friends do it, the more they believe they have the right to do it. And guess what? Thinking that's okay comes from an attitude of entitlement.

Social Media: The Good, the Bad, and the Ugly

If the Internet itself has fostered a sense of me-centrism, social media has created a frenzy of it. Sites and apps such as Facebook, Twitter, and Instagram provide instant, round-the-clock access to everyone we know (and many we don't, and don't want our kids to know, either).

Of course the benefits are wonderful. Families separated by distance can instantly see pictures of new babies and growing children, and keep up with their children and other family members. We can reconnect with old friends we'd lost touch with and find new communities. But there are dangers, too.

Self-Reflection: Are You a Social Media Role Model?

Many parents use social media every day. Think about your own use. Is it somewhat compulsive? Do you spend a lot of time on frivolous posts? If so, cutting back will model the kind of restraint you want your child to practice. Maybe you get sucked into rants and counter-rants, or hide behind an anonymous user name to blast other people. When an online exchange with a friend goes haywire, do you set a good example and make a point of talking in person instead? Today, it isn't enough for parents to practice manners when they're face to face with someone; they must also be good digital citizens and role models.

Social media sometimes brings out the worst in us. It can be used for self-promotion—boasting about our awards, our travels, or our exquisitely plated dinners. Some people say they feel depressed after viewing other people's posts. Their lives sound so ideal—their relationships so romantic, their vacations so enchanting—that they feel lonely and boring in comparison. They forget that social media posts offer only a narrow window into a life. They don't see that the vacation was a disaster except for the one moment in the picture. They don't see the fights, only the smiles. A few pictures and posts don't give us enough information to form a valid viewpoint on anyone's life. Social media is a perfect medium for encouraging entitlement:

- It lets us share mundane moments as if they were momentous occasions.
- It can overinflate the ego by providing hundreds or thousands of "friends."

- It lets us seek social support from others while giving very little back.

- It gives us the opportunity to airbrush our life to perfection. Of course, the reality can't live up to the carefully crafted image.

Then there's the Like button. For some people, this is a measurement of their self-worth. They want people—they *need* people—to "like" what they have posted. Some will post a picture and check back every few minutes to see if anyone liked it. When it is liked, they get a boost to their self-esteem; when it's not, they feel dejected. Some people have even posted negative or angry comments about their friends when they don't receive what they consider an appropriate number of likes.

An important point for kids: their online posts, photos, and videos can have a long life on the Internet, even after they've deleted them. If their posts have been forwarded, shared, or otherwise saved, they are out of the child's control.

Sometimes even fairly innocuous content can come back to haunt a person. Fernando Bryant knows this all too well. A former pro football player, he accepted a 2017 job offer as a teacher and football coach at a faith-based high school. But when parents at the school complained of an offensive social media post, the offer was rescinded. As an NBC Sports article put it, "Bryant says he's baffled. . . . The school did not tell him specifically what was posted on social media to get him fired, but he was led to believe it was a picture of himself and his wife holding a bottle of alcohol. Bryant said the school never told him employees weren't allowed to drink alcohol."[9]

Social media can feel empowering, offering a platform for voicing opinions. Of course, that's a double-edged sword.

Sometimes it's for the general good: Twitter has been known to serve a social conscience function, letting powerful people know when they've crossed a line or caused a social injustice. As such, tweets can make or break a company, or justifiably turn public opinion against a person or organization. But if used impulsively or manipulatively, tweets can be destructive as well.

In some forms, social media—and the Internet in general— allows for anonymity and abrogation of responsibility. People feel more entitled to share their opinions when they don't have to directly respond to debate or suffer any consequences. It is easy to state your belief or opinion, and then merely log off. That freedom undermines our accountability for negative impacts on others. It can also validate extreme or negative points of view. And because of the large audience, there is a high chance that even extremists will find other people who agree with them, giving them or their cause a false sense of validation.

When your child inevitably asks to use social media, you have several responsibilities as a parent:

- *Decide whether your child is ready.* Some platforms may indicate a minimum age, but it is likely unenforced. And maturity levels vary widely among children.

- *Keep watch.* Make it a clear precondition for having any social media account that you will access and view it from time to time. Spell this out in a written contract with consequences for attempts to block your access.

- *Read the rules* for each social media account to make sure privacy is set to the strictest levels. Check your child's privacy settings occasionally to be sure they haven't changed.

- *Monitor the photos* your child wants to post online, making sure they don't include telltale signs of locations and that they are not suggestive.

- *Discuss choice of words* in online posts. It's hard to read the tone of voice in a post, so play it safe. If good-natured but sarcastic banter is quoted out of context, it could sound mean, offensive, or even bullying. An ill-advised post, even if joking, can damage either your child's or their friends' reputation into the future.

Keep an open line of communication. Ask your child about how they use social media, what sites they like and why. Don't judge their responses; just listen. If you feel some of the sites are inappropriate, set some ground rules, but keep an open mind.

KEEP CALM AND DON'T LET THE JONESES BLOW YOUR COOL

Are you trying to "keep up with the Joneses"—that family who always seem to have the edge? Their home has the latest devices. Mom uses all the latest techno-gadgets, and so does her daughter. Dad wears a classic wristwatch—or the digital latest—and so does his son. Both kids always seem to have extra advantages: private school, fashion-design summer camp, sound mixing equipment in the basement. Or maybe your Joneses are free spirits who also have the means to pack up the family and sail around the world, homeschooling the kids along the way. Maybe they're the family with the second home, whether it's a cabin in the woods, a condo in Florida, or a villa in Tuscany.

— *continued* —

Whoever your Joneses are, you wish you could live up to their standards.

Or do you? Consider the following reasons to let go of your desire to keep up with the Joneses:

- *Possessions don't confer happiness.* Owning an expensive car, a large house, or the newest device might make us feel better in the short term, and might give us longer-term pleasure, too. But true happiness comes from knowing that we're living according to our values—and that doesn't depend on what we own. We may live modestly, but we can take deep satisfaction in living within our means, knowing we can pay our bills and feed our family, and teaching the habits of responsibility, gratitude, and joy to our children.

- *Appearances can deceive.* The Jones family may look awesome, but we don't know what's inside the package. Beautiful homes can house very unhappy people. These parents might be on the verge of divorce or addiction; they might worry about finances every day or have negligible relationships with their children. Fairy-tale settings do not equal fairy-tale lives. Focus on what's important to you, rather than on what you think other people have.

- *Inner resources and relationships trump outer resources and possessions.* We all need a basic level of income security. But beyond that, life satisfaction depends far more on our attitudes and our relationships. We, and in turn our children, can develop an internal sense of confidence that doesn't depend on having the newest, brightest, and best items money can buy. When our children learn that their true friends will like them, even when they don't have the newest phone, they realize their self-worth.

4

What the Future Holds

As human beings, we are all entitled to fail. It is through failure, disappointment, and conflict that we learn and grow. Success is built upon opportunities revealed by failure. But children who grow up with a sense of entitlement have often been deprived of the "right to fail." They are overpraised. Their parents often step in to solve conflicts, unwittingly robbing them of chances to challenge themselves, to find the fortitude and intelligence to work out everyday difficulties. They miss opportunities to work through relationship problems, to be forced to be productive and self-sufficient, to learn from mistakes. Kids need to be allowed to fail if they're going to learn how to succeed on their own! More on this in chapter 8, "Stop Rescuing Your Child."

For now, let's look at what the future might hold for children with an exaggerated sense of self. When your child is consistently praised for mediocre efforts, they believe that's all they need to summon up—in school, at work, in relationships, in life. They believe everyone should accept, welcome, and praise them, even when their effort is minimal. When things don't work out, the first instinct is to blame others:

- Anton's boss didn't give him a bonus this year. Anton thinks he is underappreciated and his boss is jealous of his intelligence.

- Salena got a C on a paper, but she thinks she deserves an A because she spent two nights working on it.
- Dwayne didn't get a raise at work because his work "isn't up to par"; he blames the person who trained him.
- Kara's friends frequently drift away or begin to ignore her; she believes they are all high-maintenance and difficult to get along with.
- Jamal's partner leaves him, saying he is selfish; Jamal believes when someone loves you, that person should do everything possible to make their partner happy.

For those with a me-centric worldview, everyone else is wrong. Very rarely do they look at their own behavior and take responsibility.

Entitlement strips your child's life of opportunity. It makes them resentful of other people who have more success or own more possessions. They find it hard to be happy. Your son probably doesn't know the warm feeling of gratitude. Your daughter might not feel a drive to work to succeed. Those who have a sense of entitlement frequently believe that success should simply come to them because they deserve it.

Let's take a brief look at how these attitudes might show up in different areas of life: at school, relating to others, and in the workplace. We'll also look at entitlement as a risk factor for addiction and for problems with recovery, too.

Attitudes at School

Education is a two-way street, right? The teacher needs knowledge and skill, but students must be ready and willing to learn, too. They must listen, think, and complete assignments.

Learning doesn't happen unless both teacher and student are engaged. But children who have a false sense of entitlement may lack engagement in school. While they accept that teachers have a responsibility to teach, they don't always see they also have a responsibility to learn.

> Mrs. Gallagher had a strict rule for her fifth-graders: no electronic devices in class. All devices had to be silenced and placed on her desk before class started. If anyone ignored the rule and used a device during class, Mrs. Gallagher confiscated it. For the most part, her students accepted her rule. But one day Mrs. Gallagher caught George texting under his desk, and she confiscated his phone for the remainder of the class. George was defiant. "That isn't your phone," he told her. "It's my property. You have no right to take my property." But Mrs. Gallagher kept the phone until the end of class. The next day she received a call from George's mother, who reiterated what her son had said. She insisted that Mrs. Gallagher never touch George's belongings again.

This lack of respect for authority extends from elementary school through college. As noted earlier, some college professors report that students expect good grades simply for showing up or handing in a paper, without consideration to the quality of the paper. Other students feel entitled to negotiate classroom policies, such as acceptable grounds for missing a test.

Attitudes of entitlement in the classroom don't just affect the entitled student—they can interfere with the learning environment and have a negative effect on the entire class. Students who use devices, who interrupt the teacher, or otherwise distract their classmates are ignoring the needs of those with a sincere interest in learning.

Tip: Praise Effort, Reward Results

In moderation, a promised reward can help motivate a child with a school project. But even if your child works hard on it, that doesn't mean they should be rewarded for the effort per se. Verbal praise and encouragement are perfect to let them know their efforts are noticed. But results are also important, so save any reward until the result is achieved. This ethic will prepare them for the workplace as well as in life in general.

Attitudes with Others

Close relationships are the backbone of our lives, whether with family, friends, or intimate partners. They give us support, both practically and emotionally, and should offer a safe haven. But relationships, like many other parts of life, have to be give-and-take to be satisfying for both people. When one person has a false sense of entitlement, relationships are often one-sided. The person with entitlement issues elevates their wants and needs above those of other people.

While we all have the right to *pursue* happiness, we don't all have a right to nonstop happiness. Life doesn't always go our way. Guaranteed, we'll be exasperated, depressed, or frustrated at times. But those with a sense of entitlement believe they do have a right to *be* happy. In a relationship, an entitled person believes (often unconsciously) that it's their partner's responsibility to make them happy, but their partner's happiness is not their problem. When they are dissatisfied, they often pass blame to the other person. And that's a recipe for mutual disappointment. It's impossible to maintain a healthy relationship when one person's happiness is dependent on the actions of someone else.

Sasha, a high-school senior, accepted an invitation to join several friends for a 7:30 p.m. dinner at a restaurant across town. Her friend Tanya offered to pick her up at 7:00, and Sasha readily agreed. But at 6:45, Sasha texted Tanya: she was doing errands and running late—she'd be home and ready to go by 7:30. Tanya texted back and said that wouldn't work, but Sasha could join them later at the restaurant. Instead of taking responsibility for being late, Sasha texted: "Why can't you wait half an hour? I have things to do. You are so selfish!" Tanya stood her ground, but for weeks afterward, Sasha didn't speak to her.

Whenever a family member, friend, or intimate partner doesn't prioritize the wishes of the me-centric person, that person feels neglected or shunned, like Sasha. Tanya acted respectfully and appropriately; she didn't let her boundaries get pushed. But the "slighted" person thinks they have the right to chastise, because aren't their needs more important? Besides, the other person will love them no matter what and excuse bad behavior. The truth is, however, that everyone has a right to walk away when treated poorly.

The imbalances in these relationships can show up in various ways:

- *Trust.* The person who is entitled believes their friend or partner should show trust at all times, no matter how the person has treated them. The entitled person might have lied to or betrayed their partner, but they don't see the connection between how you treat someone and how you are perceived. They believe they deserve trust without having earned it.

- *Attention.* Someone who is entitled believes they should have positive and undivided attention whenever they want it. But they aren't willing to put the same effort into other people's needs. Everyone has known a person who always calls when they want something but doesn't ever seem to be around when someone else is in need.

- *Money and things.* People who have a sense of entitlement often measure their success by possessions. They equate their worth with what and how much they own. In intimate relationships, the partner who is entitled might believe they have the right to spend joint money any way they want, regardless of whether the purchase fits into the family budget. On the other hand, they become angry when their partner chooses to do the same thing.

Successful relationships, no matter what type, are those built on mutual responsibility and respect. Both people must put forth an equal effort for the relationship to flourish. Those who are entitled frequently have relationship problems because they believe that the relationship's success is ultimately the other person's responsibility. These one-sided relationships are often filled with resentment on both sides. The person who is entitled resents the other person for not fulfilling all their needs; the partner feels resentful because they are the only person taking any responsibility.

Workplace Attitudes

As you can imagine, me-centric people enter the workforce with an inflated opinion of their abilities and their value to the workplace. They may feel they deserve honors they haven't earned, such as raises and promotions. They may view their coworkers and supervisors as too demanding. But despite their overconfidence and even bravado, they are less satisfied with their job, and more likely to underperform, pick fights with coworkers, and behave unethically than their less entitled colleagues. As millennials have entered the workforce as young adults, their older coworkers have noticed this kind of pattern.

Entitled attitudes might also figure in the "failure to launch" phenomenon—a new college graduate might keep living with their parents an extended period of time while they wait for an opportunity that they deem worthy of their skills.

> A recent college grad with a bachelor's in business, Lauren was eager to enter the corporate world, make a name for herself, and demonstrate her talents. At first, Lauren applied for manager positions, but when she was told she lacked experience, she became frustrated. Clearly, she thought, her years in college had provided her with the background she needed to be successful. These employers were not being fair or reasonable! Finally, when she started applying for entry-level jobs, she got some interviews. But in those interviews she made a bid for management positions, claiming the company should give her a chance since she was so well educated and could clearly excel as a leader.

Children who are overly praised all their lives, even for mediocre efforts, assume that employers will do the same. They find it difficult when bosses point out their faults or criticize their work. Why can't people see their innate abilities? They believe it is the employer's fault, not theirs.

Some of the other behaviors seen in entitled employees include difficulty adapting to new situations, and a tendency to be demanding or to blame others for their mistakes. They may see themselves as "above" their coworkers. They don't put forth the same effort as their coworkers because they see themselves as the benchmark that others should live up to. They expect raises and promotions simply for showing up. They are also apt to believe that they deserve recognition for doing the bare minimum because they were rewarded for the bare minimum in their youth.

Can Entitlement Be a Risk Factor for Substance Use and Addiction?

Addiction can take many forms—not only alcohol and drug use but other substances as well. Think of nicotine and even food, for example. Then there are behavioral addictions such as sex, pornography, or gambling. Recreational shopping can be habit-forming; so can Internet or social media use. When we use any substance or activity as a coping mechanism—distracting or soothing us without actually addressing our problems—the addictive potential is there. We might feel a momentary relief, but in the end we are damaging our lives.

Many addicts would never associate themselves with a sense of entitlement. In fact, many might tell you "I don't expect anything from anyone." But a false sense of entitlement can help set the stage for the development of an addiction. Unfortunately, it can also hinder recovery after a person has sought help.

How does entitlement play into addiction? Addicts—like those who feel entitled—tend to have a strong sense of how their day and life should go. When life doesn't go that way, they use it as a reason to have a drink or partake in their drug (or activity) of choice. They say many things to justify their "right" to use:

- "It was a stressful day at work."
- "Traffic was horrible/My car broke down."
- "My child is acting out."
- "My partner complains all the time."

- "My parents are always nagging me."
- "I'm nervous about that final exam—I need to relax."
- "Coach says I can't drink, but who is he to tell me what to do?"

Although addicts don't necessarily see that they are entitled, they often assume that life should be comfortable and easy. But life never goes as planned. It always has ups and downs. Stress is an ongoing feature of life. For people with entitlement issues, what might be a small problem to others is blown out of proportion. They don't have much experience handling problems; they've been rescued too often. So they use their drug or activity of choice as a buffer. And each time they do, they lose a little more of their ability to cope *without* using.

Addicts place their needs to partake in their addiction above the needs of others. Let's look at some examples:

- Wendy, a young mother, juggled caring for her two children while working part time and maintaining her household. Initially, she had a glass of wine after the children went to bed to "take the edge off." As time went on, she found that one glass wasn't enough. Soon it was half a bottle, sometimes even the whole bottle of wine. In the mornings, Sarah felt foggy, and she sometimes forgot to make sure her kids were dressed for the weather when they left for school. But Sarah's alcohol use continued. She justified it by telling herself that evenings were the only time she had for herself and that she deserved to feel good and relax.

- Trang, a college junior, had a rough day. She overslept and missed a midterm exam, then spent the afternoon in her dorm room, working on a term paper that was due the next day. When she checked her email, she learned she'd been passed over for the internship she wanted. Then her roommate came home and complained that Trang hadn't cleaned up, as she'd promised to. Trang apologized and tried to focus on her paper, but then her best friend called, angry that Trang had forgotten to return a book she'd borrowed. When she was finally done with the paper, Trang decided to relieve her stress by heading to the mall, leaving the room a mess and the borrowed book on her bed. Several hours later she arrived back at the dorm, laden with clothes worth hundreds of dollars. Her parents had given her a credit card for emergencies only—but wasn't a day like this a personal emergency? She deserved a treat, she thought, after such a tough day.

- Bill's wife asked him to come home directly after work to watch the kids because she was meeting friends for dinner. But as he left his office at six, Bill decided on a whim to stop at the casino for some quick excitement before his evening at home. I feel lucky today, he thought. I'll just play the slots for fifteen minutes. But then he didn't get home until 10 p.m.

The feeling of entitlement can compound the self-delusion of addiction. Many addicts don't believe they are like "all those other people." They don't need treatment. They don't have a problem. Other addicts can't control their habit, but they can. After all, they think, they only partake when they deserve it. (And since when are they undeserving?)

Or they might feel entitled to their addiction because no one else has a right to tell them what to do. They have the right to make decisions about their own lives, even when self-destructive. Addicts who use these types of justification never take into account that other people also have rights. They don't accept or see that their decisions affect other people. They place their "rights" to their substance of choice ahead of the rights and well-being of the people around them. When confronted with their addiction, they become angry or defensive, or they deny there is a problem.

Even in recovery, a sense of entitlement continues. Many addicts relapse because they hold on to the belief that life should be easy, comfortable, and fair. They have a hard time coping with problems because their first reaction is to see the unfairness of the situation. Despite their acceptance of their addiction, they still expect the world, and the people around them, to conform to their view of how things should work.

Successfully managing an addiction includes changing perspectives and accepting that life isn't fair, isn't easy, and doesn't always work out as planned. Full recovery can't happen until a person learns to tolerate discomfort, embrace the uncertainties of life, and see problems as an opportunity for growth.

The Mirage of Happiness

"I just want my child to be happy," is a common refrain from parents. They might give all their attention, buy their child everything they could want, and step in to make sure disappointment and hurt are kept at arm's length, all in the name of keeping a smile on the child's face. This is a recipe for entitlement. And often, it's a setup for a degree of helplessness and general dissatisfaction with life.

People who are entitled have not learned to deal with life's disappointments. As children, they could count on Mom or Dad to rescue them from an upset. Sometimes they even pre-empted a possible upset:

- Tyrone was invited to a friend's birthday party. When his parents took him shopping to buy a present, they bought Tyrone a toy, too, so he wouldn't feel bad.

- Sixteen-year-old Miriam was fired from her first job at a fast food restaurant. Her father went to see the manager to ask that his daughter be given a second chance.

- Abdul got a D on a test. He hadn't studied because he'd played in a baseball game the night before. His mother called the teacher, insisting Abdul be given a makeup test because he'd been tired from the game. She told the teacher, "Abdul's the most valuable player on the team, and he deserves a break."

Children who grow up shielded from disappointment, embarrassment, or frustration never learn to manage these emotions. Instead, they learn that they can sit back, maybe try a little bit, and someone will solve the problem for them. They are never given the chance to work through difficult situations, problem-solve, or find the inner strength to persevere. They lose the opportunity to learn about themselves and find happiness from within. Instead, they look to others to create happiness for them.

An entitled person might be in a good mood when things are going well. They feel happy when they can buy a better car than the neighbor's. They're satisfied when someone else can solve a problem for them. But that also means they're giving their capacity for happiness away. They're allowing other people's actions to control their feelings of contentment. And when they do that, they never find happiness.

We can all choose an attitude, then act on it. We can change "what's in it for me?" to "what can I do to help?" No one needs to do anything for us that we could do ourselves. Life isn't fair. Bad things happen to good people. The world doesn't owe us a happy life. We owe it to ourselves to create our own meaningful life—and then we have a chance at true happiness.

KEEP CALM, LOOK AHEAD, AND PARENT ON

The decisions you make today will affect your child's future. With each day, your child's character is taking shape, and you can influence that shape. Young children think of the present moment. It is up to you to factor the future into your child-raising decisions, to weigh the implications. When facing a choice, consider which choice will teach a lesson that will benefit your son or daughter in adulthood. Let's say your son wants to go to a friend's house and assures you he will do his (long-delayed) chores tomorrow. As an adult, will it be better for him to shirk responsibilities in order to have fun or to understand that fun comes after obligations are met?

As you learn to say no to your child, ignore your own pain and discomfort. Watching your child suffer disappointment may make you squirm, may even make you feel genuine suffering. But somehow, for their future, you have to hide your pain, put it aside and parent on. As your child gains in wisdom and good judgment, your discomfort will be richly rewarded.

We encourage our children to make the right decisions but continue to love them even when they make poor choices. That doesn't mean they aren't going to sometimes suffer the consequences, but it will mean they know they are accepted and loved, no matter what.

Change Yourself, Change Your Child

Part 2

5

Change Yourself, Change Your Child

On summer Saturday evenings, the neighbors on Buttonwood Street often gathered informally on a porch or stoop as their school-age children played together. One evening, their conversation led to the topic of spoiled attitudes. One of the mothers, a manager at a local insurance firm, talked about a recent college graduate her company had hired. During his first several months, he'd often arrived late and missed deadlines. Even so, he had asked his manager for a raise, apparently believing that the company should be thankful that he chose to work there. Next, a father in the group mentioned that his three middle-schoolers wanted only their favorite foods at dinner. Otherwise, they'd refuse to eat, forcing either him or his spouse back into the kitchen to make several different meals. Another mother lamented about how materialistic her young teens were, constantly whining for the newest skateboard, the latest video game, or the phone "all their friends have."

One dad wondered aloud what had caused this epidemic. All the parents chimed in. One blamed the schools for not giving enough homework or having lower standards than when they were kids. Another blamed toy companies for the bombardment of ads kids are exposed to. One father blamed society in general for coddling kids, making them expect a handout. But what nobody mentioned was their own parenting styles and attitudes. These neighbors all agreed that something must be done, but what? *They* couldn't do anything, if everyone else was to blame.

But guess what? If you're seeing entitled attitudes in your kid, *you* are primarily to blame. That's right, you—the one who applies the rules inconsistently, who waffles when your child shirks chores, who doesn't model gratitude, who makes empty threats your kid can see through. But here's the good news. If you're to blame, that means you've got lots of influence. That means you can use that influence to make some changes. Whether you're seeing early signs of consistent selfishness in your toddler or full-blown entitlement issues in your teen, it *is* possible to change your child. But you must first change yourself.

And isn't changing yourself and committing to it the most challenging exercise of all? Setting a limit is easy; maintaining a limit is much more difficult. As you read this book, take the time to honestly look at your approach to parenting. Understand that your child has learned their attitudes from you, and it is from you that they can unlearn them. The good news is that once you start making heartfelt, consistent changes, it often doesn't take long for you to see changes in your child.

Read these statements and decide if this is something you might say to a trusted friend:

- "At least once a day I feel like I can't go through one more battle with my child."
- "I regularly give in to my child's requests (such as fudging bedtime, allowing food when it's off limits, buying treats

at the checkout line) because it's easier than having an argument."

- "I often feel like I need a break from my daughter."
- "I dream about taking a vacation—without my son."
- "I find myself saying no constantly."
- "Occasionally I've avoided spending time with family or friends because I'm embarrassed about my child's behavior."
- "I feel like I'm always nagging my child."
- "I worry that my child is a spoiled brat."

If you found yourself agreeing with several of these statements, join the club—the club of well-intentioned but (let's face it) wimpy parents. You could probably benefit from making at least some changes to how you are parenting.

Why Children Misbehave

Your child wants your attention, and they'll go to great lengths to make sure you notice them. Your attention is their reward, and when you reward a behavior, you'll see that behavior again. Here's the catch: that's true whether your attention is positive or negative, whether it is affection or punishment.

> Whenever three-year-old Annie didn't get her way, she fell on the floor and cried. Her exasperated mother, Monica, didn't know what to do. It was especially embarrassing when Annie threw a fit in public, like she had the week before when she'd wanted a toy horse she saw at the store. At those times, Monica tended to give in, just to get her child off the floor. At home, Monica often punished Annie for this behavior, sending her to her room or for a time out. But even at home

she sometimes gave in. So Annie has learned that if she fell on the floor and cried, there was a good chance she'd get what she wanted. For her, it was a winning strategy because each time she did it, her mother paid some kind of attention to her, and often gave in to her wants, too. Monica was rewarding Annie for falling on the floor and crying.

Our children do exactly what we teach them to do. They will behave or not behave—whatever works to get them their desired result. Annie uses the behavior she knows will work. Her experience shows it's a good strategy. By responding inconsistently to Annie's crying fits, Monica is unfortunately giving us an example of the principle of "intermittent reinforcement." When Annie gets what she wants—which is most

---

Self-Reflection: Are You Overcompensating?

Sometimes parents fall into a pattern of intermittent reinforcement as a result of overcompensating for their own perceived shortcomings. If you feel guilty about working late and missing dinner, that night you might give in to your child's demand to stay up later, even though she'll be tired at school the next day. If you're ill and can't give your child attention, instead you might give in and order a new toy for him when he whines for it. When you feel guilty, you overcompensate; when you don't, you enforce the rules. So at any time, your child might hope he can beat the rules this time.

Does this dynamic sound familiar? If you're inconsistent in enforcing boundaries and rules, ask yourself whether you're trying to make up for what you consider a weakness in parenting. Whatever your errors as a parent—and we're probably all doing our best—remember that your child is best served by consistency.

---

of the time—the behavior is reinforced. She may not get it, but it's worth a gamble. It's like using a slot machine—it may not always pay out, but you keep pulling the lever, knowing that eventually you'll hit the jackpot. Even when Annie is punished for her behavior, she has learned that if she doesn't give up, she will eventually get her payday. It's worth noting that behaviors learned through intermittent reinforcement are among the hardest to change.

Four Steps to Changing Your Child's Behavior

Intermittent reinforcement or not, here's the key to changing your child's behavior: you must actively *teach* them how you'd like them to act. You do that by modeling the behavior you want to see, changing your reactions to the bad behavior, teaching them step-by-step instructions for the new behavior, and then—this is important—letting natural consequences flow from their behavior, both good and bad. Let's look at each step of that process.

Model the Behavior You Want to See

Actions speak louder than words. It's a truism, and never more true than with parents and children. They will imitate your behavior even if you give lip service to the opposite. For example, suppose you want your child to practice good manners by saying please, thank you, and you're welcome. The first step is to be sure *you* are using these words regularly. Do you say please when you ask your partner to answer the doorbell? Do you say thank you when your child helps you with your grocery bags? Every day we have many opportunities to be polite—to the supermarket cashier, a server at your neighborhood eatery, the driver who lets you go first at the stop sign, your partner when they bring you a glass of water, or your child when you ask them to clean up their toys. If you automatically use good manners, your child will too. If you skip over these pleasantries, no matter how often you ask your child to use them, they'll skip over them, too. In short, make sure you are modeling the behavior you want your child to use.

This works for just about every behavior. Do you want your child to understand that they can't have whatever they want, whenever they want it? Then make sure you mention that you're planning to buy a new sofa, but you have to save money for it first. If you want your child to feel appreciation, be sure to express *your* appreciation for the people and things in your life. If you want your child to show kindness toward others, you must show kindness to others. Whatever behaviors you believe your child is lacking, look first at yourself to make sure you are setting the right example.

Change Your Reactions

It's not easy. Your child might have spent years behaving in certain ways to get what they want. Now you're undermining their tried-and-true systems! They will continue to test you, using their old patterns and expecting the same result. They may rebel, get angry, or refuse to cooperate when you don't react the way you used to. But eventually, if a behavior no longer works, they will try a different one.

It won't happen overnight, but your goal is to create an environment where your child has their needs—emotional and physical—met by their own responsible behavior. You want to show your daughter that she is in control. By her own action, she gets to choose whether you respond positively. If she says please, you'll tie her shoelaces. If there's no please, then no help with the shoelaces. She is in control of the outcome. Your job is to be consistent: to respond positively when she acts appropriately, and to ignore demanding, whiny, or entitled behavior.

Parent Challenge: Introduce Change a Bit at a Time

Choose one behavior you want to change at a time. Let's say your goal is consistent use of please and thank you. Start by explaining to your child that your expectations have changed. You might say, "You're getting older, and it's time to think about better manners. When you ask for something, say please and thank you. If you want some juice, please say, 'Mom, can I please have some juice?' Once I give you the juice, you say, 'Thank you.' I won't do what you want until you ask properly."

The key to changing any behavior is consistency. You must respond the same way each time. If your child doesn't say please, withhold the juice! Your child will catch on and start saying please. But first, your reaction must change consistently.

Teach the Right Behavior

It isn't enough to simply tell your child what you expect. Sometimes you must teach the steps needed. Suppose your son has a habit of interrupting you. Whether you're on the phone, vacuuming, or talking with your partner, your child simply stands in front of you and demands that you pay attention. You could say, "It isn't polite to interrupt me," but that only tells him what *not* to do, it doesn't tell him what to do.

So give step-by-step instructions. You might say, "When you want my attention and I'm busy, I'd like you to come and gently tap me and say, 'excuse me.' If you do that, I will listen to what you need to say. If you don't say 'excuse me,' I'll continue what

I'm doing." Now, go through the motions with your child. You gently tap him and say, "excuse me," and then have him do the same to you. When you both tell and show him, he will better understand exactly what you want.

You have now told your child what you expect and how you will react. Once you have explained exactly how you want your child to behave, don't accept anything less. Don't pour the juice for your daughter until she says please. Don't stop what you're doing to pay attention to your son unless he taps you gently and says, "excuse me." If your child forgets, remind them. Be consistent in only accepting this new behavior.

Phrase your request as "please do this," rather than "don't do that." When your child gets up from the table and leaves their dirty dish, "please take your plate to the sink" is more effective than "don't leave your plate on the table." Positive statements receive more attention from your child.

You might worry that a bad habit is ingrained, and it's too late to change their behavior. It isn't. Your child, no matter how old, wants your attention and your love. While it's true that you cannot force someone to change their behavior, you can always change your reaction to it. The more you expect and reinforce a certain behavior, the more you will get it.

Tip: Give Clear Instructions

Be as specific as possible. Vagueness is a recipe for disappointment. Your son's idea of cleaning his room might be very different from yours. So make a checklist of what it means to clean a room: make the bed, put dirty clothes in the hamper, pick up books and games from the floor, and so on. The more specific your expectations, the easier it is for your child to meet them.

Let the Consequences Flow

Sometimes we want to protect our child from the consequences of their poor decisions. We see these as punishments, or we believe that everyone is entitled to make mistakes and our kids shouldn't suffer because of it. But natural consequences teach important lessons. In the adult world, nobody can protect you from getting fired because you were late too often or because you undermined your boss. Nobody will bail you out of a financial bind because you carelessly went over your budget.

Your child must learn the natural consequences that result from their behavior. You can teach this lesson from a young age, such as having them finish dinner before having dessert. But as the consequences become more serious, we often want to jump in and solve the situation, by bringing a forgotten homework assignment to school or staying up late to finish a science project your child abandoned.

> Twelve-year-old Katrina planned to go to the movies with her friend on Saturday afternoon. Her dad, Jorge, said she could go as long as she cleaned her room first. He'd drive her, and they'd pick Nedira up on the way. Katrina woke up late that morning and then watched television. She knew she needed to clean her room, but kept putting off the task even though her dad reminded her. Before she knew it, it was time to leave and she hadn't yet cleaned her room. Jorge refused to take her. Katrina was angry. "How can you do this?" she snapped. "You promised I could go! Nedira is waiting for us!" She stormed into her room and slammed the door. Even though he felt guilty, Jorge held his ground. He called Nedira's mom to explain. Then he told Katrina she could go to the movies the following weekend if she cleaned her room first. The next Saturday, Katrina woke up early and had her room cleaned hours before it was time to go.

Jorge let Katrina feel the natural consequences of her decision. He knew that as Katrina becomes an adult, the consequences of shirking responsibility will be more severe. She has to learn that if you don't do your homework, you'll fail a class; if you ignore your deadlines at work, you'll lose the job. Much as Jorge wanted to give in and let Katrina go to the movies, he knew that in the long term that lenience wouldn't benefit her. He opted to teach her that actions have consequences and show that Katrina herself is in control of the consequences—both good and bad—because she controls her actions and choices.

The same is true when your daughter calls from school and asks you to bring the report she forgot at home, or her sneakers for after-school sports. Try just letting the natural consequences flow. If she forgets her report, she won't get credit for it. If she forgets her sneakers, she doesn't get to participate in athletics that day. When you drop everything to bring forgotten items to school, you're taking away your child's ability to learn from those mistakes. More on this in chapter 11, "Stop Rescuing Your Child."

Tip: Sometimes Nobody's At Fault

In everyday situations, kids do have control over their own actions and the resulting consequences. But sometimes bad things happen that are nobody's fault. As a parent, you need to know the difference. If your teen driver is in a car accident even though he was being careful, or an item is stolen even though your child took appropriate steps to safeguard it, then feel free to step in and provide help and support. It's your job as a parent to know the difference, helping when necessary but generally letting them deal with the consequences of their own behavior.

Change takes effort. We're often motivated to change only when we realize we must—when we realize that our child's true emotional needs are not being met and neither are ours! It's not your duty to forego your needs to make your child's life more pleasant in the moment. Healthy families take everyone's needs into consideration.

KEEP CALM AND "BE THE CHANGE"

Our actions today help shape both our and our children's tomorrows. Let these ideas guide you:

- *Be the change you wish to see in the world.* Whether Gandhi actually said those words or not, the message is powerful. As a parent, you are a primary shaping influence on your child. Let your own behavior speak.

- *Everyone wants to be loved and recognized.* Your child will behave or misbehave based on which gets them the attention they want. New behaviors aren't learned instantaneously. It takes time and patience, but in the end it is worthwhile.

- *Natural consequences are the best teacher.* Let your child feel the natural consequences of their behavior, both good and bad. They're more effective than any words you could use—and they take you out of the equation.

6

Respect

MODEL IT, TEACH IT

One day in July, Tomas stopped home during his lunch hour to see his fifteen-year-old daughter Eliza. He wanted to check on her progress with a list of chores she'd been given. Eliza was sitting on the couch watching television and texting her friends. "What chores did you do this morning?" Tomas asked, even though he could see the answer — the breakfast dishes were still in the sink, the floors weren't vacuumed, and the laundry was still in the basket by the stairs, untouched.

"I haven't started yet," Eliza replied, sounding annoyed that he was asking. "I'll get around to them, but I don't have anything to do all week so I have plenty of time."

Tomas walked over, turned off the television, and took his daughter's phone. "When I get home later, you can have the phone back if all your chores are done."

Angrily, Eliza told her dad he was overreacting. She would get around to the chores. "Why does it matter when they get done?" She huffed and walked away.

Tomas called after her that she needed to show more respect to him. He kept the phone and returned to his office. All afternoon he wondered how and when Eliza had become so disrespectful.

• • •

Merriam-Webster defines *respect* as "a feeling or understanding that someone or something is important, serious, etc., and should be treated in an appropriate way." Although it's a useful definition, it doesn't explain the "appropriate way," leaving it up for discussion. Have you taught your child what *you* mean by the word *respect*? What kinds of respect would you like your child to show to everyone? Are there other kinds of respect you consider appropriate for authority figures? It's worth thinking about.

Self-Reflection:
Consider Your Own Respect for Authority Figures

Think back over your life and your interactions with other people, especially those in authority—your parents, teachers, bosses, legal or government authorities. Think about your childhood, teens, and adulthood. Did you show respect—or not? What interactions come to mind as somehow revealing? Write them down. What in the situation influenced how you acted? How did your actions make you feel afterward? You are your child's first and most significant authority figure. Your child will emulate the attitude you have toward authority. If you show respect, they will learn to show respect. If not, it will be a hard lesson for you to teach.

Teaching Respect

We may feel that we know respect (and disrespect) when we see it, but it's a bit hard to define precisely. So let's start with what it typically looks like. In American society, we do have some basic behaviors we see as a sign of respect:

- being responsible; being true to our word
- being generous and sharing

- offering other people help when needed
- listening to others
- tolerating differences
- apologizing for mistakes
- using common courtesy and polite language
- allowing other people privacy
- following instructions of those in authority
- taking care of other people's property

We also have an idea of how disrespectful behavior looks:

- not following through on promises; being irresponsible
- being argumentative
- being dismissive or sarcastic
- ignoring others who need help
- being unapologetic after making a mistake
- intruding on other people's business

Family Activity: Spotting Respect

When your family is out in public—perhaps in your community or on an outing—try looking for examples of respect and disrespect. Set a goal of finding ten of each.

That's respect:
- holding the door for the person behind you
- using a public wastebasket for trash
- thanking a store clerk

That's disrespect:
- leaving dog waste on the sidewalk
- being rude to a waitress
- cutting into the front of the line to get on the bus

- being unmannerly or rude to others; using foul language
- treating other people's possessions carelessly

As parents, we want our children to choose behaviors from the "respectful" list. But let's first make sure we take the time to teach and show them *how* to act respectfully, and let's set some consequences for not acting that way.

Define What Respect Means to You

If you find yourself telling your child "you need to learn some respect," it's possible you and your child have different interpretations of the word. (It's similar to telling a child to take care of the dog. What do you mean: give the dog food and water, and take him for a walk? Play with him in the yard? Bathe and brush him? You'd better be clear.) When you and your spouse or co-parent have different definitions, you have different expectations.

Parent Challenge: What Does Respect Look Like?

Sit down with your partner and talk about what respect means to each of you. (If you're a single parent or divorced, you can do this exercise alone, or consider involving others as appropriate.) Together, create a list of behaviors you expect of your child to show respect. Review the list to make sure your own behaviors match what you've written; if not, change your own behavior starting now. Decide the consequences when your child doesn't act with respect. Finally, use the list to talk about respect with your child. You are no longer leaving the word up for interpretation; you are giving them a clear roadmap on how to act.

When you know exactly what being respectful means to you, it's easier to correct minor problems rather than letting them slide because your child isn't feeling well or completely ignoring them to avoid an argument. You can point to the list, explain how your child acted disrespectfully, and institute the consequence you already decided on with your partner. Not only does your child have a roadmap for how to act, you do as well.

Parent or Friend? Don't Try to Be Both

Sure, we want our children to like us, trust us, and tell us what is going on in their life. Some parents feel the best way to do this is to become their friend. It isn't. When you become your child's friend, you elevate them to a false equality. You tell them their opinion matters as much as yours does. You take away your right to give your child guidance, make rules, and set limits. Family, much to the chagrin of some parenting philosophies, is a hierarchal structure. Parents need to establish that hierarchy, and kids need to respect it.

As we noted in chapter 2, a parent's job is both emotional and functional. You are there to love, support, and encourage your child. That's the emotional part. You are there to set and enforce limits and household rules, and to provide housing, safety, food, and clothing. That's the functional part. Parenting doesn't work when you only provide one of the two. Children who grow up without love are at greater risk of substance abuse and emotional problems throughout their life. Children with inadequate care for their physical needs are at risk of both physical and emotional problems. Parents offer both emotional and functional support. Friends don't.

That's not to say parents can't develop strong and close bonds with their children. They can and should. But parents shouldn't burden their children with their relationship woes or financial problems. You're seeing these situations from an adult perspective, but your child doesn't have the emotional maturity to process adult information. You are not on equal footing with your child. You need the upper hand. Parents don't need their child to like them; they need their child to *respect* them.

> Elyssa was watching television with her eight-year-old son, Sean. It was almost his bedtime, and she reminded him that when the show was over, he needed to go to bed. For the next few minutes, they laughed and talked together. After a long day at work, Elyssa enjoyed this closeness. "Mommy, you're my best friend," Sean said. She was touched and told Sean that he's her best friend as well. When the show ended, Sean wanted to stay up longer and watch another one together. Elyssa wanted this "friendship" to last, so instead of insisting on bedtime, she agreed Sean could stay up.

Yes, you want a parent-child relationship built on love, mutual trust, companionship, and open communication. But in doing so, the parent also needs to stay in charge. Young children and teens need to know they can trust their parents to care for them, be supportive when there is a problem, and believe in them—and also give them the limits they need to feel safe (whether they'd admit that or not).

Self-Reflection: Parent or Friend? It's Personal

If you have a need to be your child's friend, take a step back to think about why. Maybe your own parents were distant from you—could you be overcorrecting now? Maybe you're lonely and need a friend yourself. Maybe you reflexively want your child to always like you. (Why might that be?) Maybe you believe that you've somehow wronged your child—through neglect or because of your own needs. You want to restart the relationship, but aren't sure you have the right to act like a parent.

Parenting is different from friendship. Friends are on equal footing, sharing affection and interests, often with similar viewpoints and values. If you behave more like a friend than a parent, you forfeit your priceless role as teacher, coach, and setter of limits and expectations. You tell your child you two are equal when you are not.

Once you've reflected on this question, take steps outside of your relationship with your child to resolve the issue. Then work on ways to become a parent rather than a friend.

Too often, parents fall into the trap of sharing too much information with their child because they want an open relationship. They might tell the child that they believe a teacher is being unfair, or that an uncle is exasperating, or that they don't like the neighbor down the street. But children don't have the emotional maturity or experience to process this burdensome information. For example, they might not understand that your anger at the neighbor was momentary; now you've solved the problem and are once again neighborly.

It's certainly acceptable for parents to share their own feelings at times: "I'm disappointed we won't be able to take a vacation this year," or "I feel nervous when I meet new people, too." Sharing feelings can go a long way toward building trust. But first ask yourself whether the sharing might cause distress, whether it veers into non-age-appropriate subjects, and whether it might reflect badly on others (especially the other parent).

It's hard to switch between being a friend and a parent.

Imagine spending time talking with your teenage daughter Nailah about her circle of friends. You might be tempted to share your own friendship dramas with Nailah—even some details about her friends' mothers—but think for a moment. In a few hours you may need to insist that Nailah finish her homework. Once you cross the line to friendship, it is difficult to regain your control as parent. Remember, your job as a parent is more like a coach's role. You are there to guide their values, provide them the skills they need to be independent, and instill the confidence for them to be successful. Your job is not to be their confidante—or to turn them into yours.

Parent Challenge: Upgrade Yourself from Friend to Parent

If you notice that you are confiding in your child or talking about inappropriate topics (household finances or your own relationship issues), you should stop. It's too much information for your child and can cause worries and possibly problems in their future relationships.

Talk to your child. Let them know you've decided not to discuss certain topics with them (name those topics in general terms) simply because it's not right for a parent to share on those subjects; the child is not at fault. Tell them you'd much rather talk about other things—and name a few of those, too.

If you need to, reach out to other adults to talk to about the issues.

Think of the relationship between a boss and employee. As the employee, you can be friendly with your boss. You can share stories, compare opinions about world events, enjoy each other's company, and be genuinely concerned about one another. But within the relationship, there is still the knowledge that one person is in charge. The parent-child relationship is similar: you can love one another, share stories, spend time together, and develop a close bond as long as you, as the parent, stay in charge.

Consider This: Respect Is a Key to Success

Children who fail to learn respect will face struggles all their life. They will likely be poor friends, partners, and employees. Respect is the cornerstone of all relationships.

Teaching Respect

Teaching your child how to act involves several steps: modeling the behavior by both explaining and showing them how to act, implementing consequences for inappropriate behavior, and praising appropriate behavior. Try using those steps as you teach the following respectful behaviors:

- *Be polite.* Use please, thank you, you're welcome, and excuse me/pardon me in your house regularly. While it might sometimes feel monotonous or a bit formal, it's worth it. Home is where these essential pleasantries become a habit, and your child is more likely to use them outside your house. If child gets away with inappropriate manners at home, the habit will not form.

- *Express negative emotions in a positive way.* Frustration and anger are normal human emotions; You can't stop your child from feeling negative emotions; however, you can teach them to express them in a different way. Saying "let's talk about how you're feeling" works better than "you shouldn't get angry at your brother."

- *Use conversation skills.* Explain the importance of being a good listener. When your child needs you, put down your cell phone and give them your undivided attention. And expect your child to do the same. During family conversations, practice taking turns talking, not inter-rupting, and asking questions about what the other person has said. Always use a calm, respectful voice when setting limits.

- *Follow household rules.* Include rules such as no hitting, no name-calling, clean up after yourself, and respecting others. You might need to remind your child of what you mean when you say *respect.* This helps prepare your child for school, college, and the work world. There are always rules we all must follow and consequences for ignoring them.

- *Practice tolerance.* Teach your child that they will meet people they don't like and that not everyone is going to like them, but it is never okay to be mean. They should treat everyone with respect, even when they don't agree with them. Teach your child not to judge someone based on how they look, where they live, what church they go to, or who they love, reminding them that even though there are differences, we are all the same on the inside. Read stories or watch movies about different religions, cultures, and lifestyles to give your child an accepting view of the world.

- *Plan ahead.* Talk with your child about expectations when you are approaching situations in which they might act inappropriately or disrespectfully. For example, before going to a restaurant, explain your expectations of their behavior and remind them to use good manners.

- *Be respectful to others.* Modeling appropriate behavior is very important. Your child learns more from how you act than from what you say. Remember to include respect for other people's property, too.

As you're teaching your child about respect, it helps to remember:

- *Review your expectations and revise as needed.* Make sure your expectations match your child's age and abilities. Revise when needed, for example, suppose you are going to a lengthy event. Decide whether it is appropriate to expect your son to sit quietly through the entire event or if he can bring some toys or a tablet to keep himself occupied.

- *Keep your child's behavior in perspective.* If your daughter yells at a friend or calls them a name, don't take it personally. If your teen acts disrespectful to you, don't take it personally. These are normal childhood behaviors. While you want to bring attention to the behavior and set consequences should it continue, you shouldn't see it as an affront against you or your parenting skills. It is important to remember that children are not "mini-adults," and therefore will act like children. Don't expect them to act like adults; instead, they should be respectful children.

- *Make sure you and your partner are working together.* If both parents have different expectations, it will end up confusing your child. Review your expectations with your partner, and if there are differences, resolve them privately to provide your child with consistency.

KEEP CALM AND CHANNEL YOUR INNER DRILL SERGEANT

You may not have the soul of a drill sergeant, but face it: in your home, you lay down the law. Still, your family life need not feel like boot camp. To keep the sweat and the drama to a minimum, keep it simple, with clear rules and agreed-on consequences. (Later, in the teens, negotiation can have a limited role: see chapter 15, "Declarations of Independence.")

Do you see drill sergeants pleading with their soldiers? No. So don't get in the habit of begging or pleading with your child to do something; this gives them the impression that they have power in the situation. Simply let them know what consequences will apply if your requests go unheeded.

Always follow through on consequences, both positive and negative. Respect for a parent is only as good as the parent's word. If you waver from what you said, your child will lose respect.

Children will have many friends over the course of their life; they will only have one set of parents. Avoid "downgrading" yourself to a friend when you have a much more valuable role as a parent.

7

Gratitude Takes Practice

Coming home from visiting a friend, five-year-old Sadie told her mother about the friend's dollhouse. "I want one, too!" she said. Sylvia wished she could afford it, but knew it wasn't in her budget. For weeks Sadie talked about the dollhouse, drew pictures of it, and complained that playing with her dolls wasn't any fun because they didn't have a house. Sylvia sighed and started putting money aside. After several months she had enough, and for Sadie's birthday, she surprised her with a dollhouse. At first Sadie was excited. But within days she'd pushed it to a corner of her bedroom, and there it sat, ignored. Sadie told her mother about a new toy she had seen on television. That, she said, was so much better than the dollhouse.

• • •

Sadie, like many children, expects her parents to give in to every whim. They don't understand that toys, like clothes, food, and rent, cost money and money can be scarce. Rather than appreciating what they have, they often focus on what they don't have.

Why Gratitude Matters

"Grateful people experience high levels of positive emotions such as joy, enthusiasm, love, happiness, and optimism," says author Robert Emmons. "The practice of gratitude as a discipline protects a person from the destructive impulsive of envy, resentment, greed, and bitterness. We have discovered that a person who experiences gratitude is able to cope more effectively with everyday stress, may show increased resilience in the face of trauma-induced stress and may recover more quickly from illness and benefit from greater physical health."[10]

Consider This: Gratitude Has Superpowers

Being grateful has many positive impacts. In a study published in 2008, one group of middle school students wrote down five things they were grateful for; a second group wrote down five gripes, complaints, or hassles. Not surprisingly, the group that focused on gratefulness was found to have a better outlook on school and greater life satisfaction at a three-week follow-up.[11] A 2012 study showed that teens who are grateful are more likely to be happy, less likely to abuse drugs and alcohol, and less likely to have behavior problems.[12]

Gratitude, it turns out, is good for us both emotionally and physically through the whole lifespan. People who practice gratitude in their everyday life have a greater sense of well-being. They may have better health, more friends, and go further in their careers. But throughout our life, we too often focus on what's broken or what we lack. We forget to be appreciative for what we have.

Sam stopped at the grocery store to pick up a few items for his family. He was on a strict budget until payday on Friday, but they needed food for another meal or two. Sam picked out a bag of frozen ravioli, a jar of sauce, a loaf of bread, and a dozen eggs. As he stood in the checkout line, he watched the family in front of him unload their groceries onto the conveyer belt. There was a steak, shrimp, fresh vegetables, a bag of apples. Sam looked at his groceries, wishing he could afford to shop like that. Suddenly he felt immense disappointment in himself and the few items in his basket. He went home grumbling instead of feeling appreciative that his family would have food for the rest of the week.

It's easy to look at what other people have and assume their life is better because of what they own. Maybe your neighbor's new car makes you look at your old one with disdain. But if you cop to that attitude, you're telling your kid to save their thankfulness for later, when they get that desired item. Instead, try conveying the message—ideally by example—that thankfulness is something to practice each day.

During the Thanksgiving holiday, many families take the time to talk about what they appreciate. But for gratefulness to add benefit to our life, we need to be thankful every day, for both the big and small things in life.

Teaching the Skill of Gratitude

Although we might see gratitude as an emotion, it is really a skill—to teach, practice, and master. If we view gratitude as an emotion, we're likely to assume that your child either has it or doesn't. Emotions can't be taught; you can't instruct your child to be happy or sad. Gratitude is different. See it as a critical life and social skill. It *is* something you can teach your child.

Even young children can have a sense of gratitude. It might seem impossible to teach a toddler or preschooler how to appreciate the things and people in their lives. At this age, children are me-centered, and this is developmentally appropriate. They are exploring their worlds and learning that they are separate beings from their parents. But even toddlers can learn to say thank you when it's called for. When you expect children to show appreciation from a young age, the feeling of appreciation follows.

Children don't have an adult perspective on life. They don't understand budgets. They don't realize that parents also have needs, and sometimes those needs come before theirs. They don't have the benefit of knowing history, and that previous generations didn't have the luxuries we have today. They haven't learned about children growing up in worn-torn countries or places without running water, medical care, or enough food. They see the world they were born into, and until they learn otherwise, they assume everyone lives the same way they do.

Tip: What Teens and Toddlers Have in Common

Developmentally, toddlers and preschoolers are focused on *me* and *mine;* they don't have much capacity for appreciation and gratitude yet. That capacity increases as the child grows, but you might see this all-about-me attitude appear again in the teen years, when the desire for independence blossoms. This me-centric stage is developmentally appropriate for teens, as it is with young children. But by this age, your teen should have some ingrained habits of politeness to offset some of the self-centered focus. You can also balance this second me-centric phase by having your teen participate in volunteer work and community service.

How then, can children learn to appreciate the basic, yet wonderful things in life—the fact that they have a safe home with a reliable food supply, that you made their lunch before school, that there's a school down the street or a bus to pick them up? To children, these wonders are simply normal. Too often, we reserve gratefulness for the *extras* in life. And the more we give our children, the more they may see those extras as normal. If your family takes a beach vacation every year, they're likely to take it for granted rather than seeing it as a treat to be extra grateful for.

Gratitude begins with you. Before trying to teach your child appreciation, look at yourself. Are you grateful, and do you express it? Try showing your appreciation for everyday things:

- "I really enjoyed spending time with you today."
- "It is great that your friend came over to play."
- "What a delicious meal. Thank you for cooking."
- "What a wonderful surprise!"
- "It's raining today—doesn't it feel good to be warm and dry at home?"

It is our attitude as well as our words that teach our children to appreciate both the big and the small things in life. Teaching gratitude means modeling it consistently.

Parent Challenge: Five Things I'm Thankful For

Flex your own gratitude muscle. Each day for the next thirty days, write down five things that make you feel grateful. As you make your daily list, review what you've written on past days. As the month progresses, you may notice that your perspective changes. You might even purposefully look for things or people you appreciate. You might also want to gauge or rate your feelings of happiness, well-being, and optimism. How do these change over the thirty days?

As your child grows and attends school, they'll learn about countries where children don't have enough to eat or don't have medicines when they are sick. It is hard for privileged kids to imagine that there are people who live without electricity in their home, or who are hungry or cold. So, in age-appropriate ways, expose your child to these realities, through books, television, and real life. Of course you don't want to overwhelm your kindergartener with pictures of starving children or make them feel guilty about eating their dinner. Take their age and their temperament into account. The point is to increase their feelings of gratitude and to instill in them a desire to help others who are less fortunate.

Even your daily comments can make a difference. For example, rather than saying "you have to go to school," change it to "you *get* to go to school." You're showing that going to school isn't a chore or punishment, but rather a privilege.

And then there's consumerism and the advertising messages that pervade our lives. Partner these messages with our need for instant gratification—*I want it now*—and it makes sense that appreciating what we have can become an ever-more elusive skill. In today's fast-paced commerce, many children learn that everything is literally available at our fingertips. With a few impulsive clicks, we can have anything delivered right to our door. But when we don't have to work for that purchase, when we don't choose it carefully or save for weeks or months for it,

---

Family Activity: Gratitude Jar

Place a jar somewhere that is easily accessible to everyone in the family. Put a small pad of paper and a pencil next to the jar. Have family members write down one thing they are grateful for each day and put the paper in the jar. Once a week, sit down together, maybe during a family dinner, and read aloud the slips of paper.

---

we simply don't have the same appreciation for it. Rather than looking around with thankfulness at all our belongings, we take them for granted and want more.

To help your child learn gratefulness and show appreciation in a consumer-based world, you might try the following:

- Have your child do extra work around the house—beyond any regular chores—to earn what they want.

- If you give an allowance, have your child save part of it each time toward a purchase.

- When your child wants something, explain that they must wait until their birthday, the holidays, or a time when your family normally gives gifts.

When your child is involved in the "getting" part of the process, he will have a greater appreciation of the item. Delayed gratification, the anticipation of and working for something, all add to the value of an item. When you have more than you can use, you take things for granted; it becomes difficult to hold onto a feeling of gratitude. But when you put forth an effort, when everything around you has meaning and is a source of pride, you gain a sense of appreciation.

Receiving Gifts Gracefully

Any parent would feel mortified if their child opened a present and said, "I already have this" or "this isn't what I wanted!" We want our children to receive gifts graciously. We want them to feel, and show, appreciation for the giver—even if the present's not an absolute hit. Accepting presents and compliments is a skill, and like other life skills, you can teach your child how to gracefully receive a gift.

It Is the Thought That Counts

When a child receives a gift, they tend to focus on the item itself. It's easy to show appreciation and excitement when it's exactly what they wanted. But we've all seen a child's face fall after they rip the paper off a present only to find a sweater, a pair of pajamas, or an unwanted toy. It's hard for them to hide their disappointment. Both the child and the gift-giver feel let down.

> Keith wanted a toy robot for his sixth birthday. He told every-one he saw—his parents, his grandparents, his friends—about the robot; he watched the TV ad with rapt attention. At his birthday party, several presents were waiting for him. First his grandparents handed him a big box. Keith thought it could be the robot! But when he opened it and found a fire truck, he yelled, "I hate fire trucks!" He threw it aside and tore open the other gifts until he found the robot. His parents were embarrassed, and his grandparents looked hurt.

It's not until we're older that we realize the item itself is insignificant. What matters is the thought behind the gift, the sentiment that moved the person to give it. When we say thank you, we are thanking the person for caring about us. Sure, we all get presents that we're unenthused about: the handmade sweater from Aunt Edna, the tool we already own. But we find a way to show our appreciation, and we *do* appreciate the sentiment. It can be a difficult balance for an adult; for children it's even harder.

You're thinking, but I don't want to teach my child to lie. Yes, honesty is good. How then do you justify telling your child to say they love a gift, even when they don't? Some parents might say that little white lies are okay, if they're said to protect the other person's feelings. But there are ways we can show appreciation without saying we adore a gift we don't. It's called courtesy or tact. Provide your child with a few handy phrases:

- "I don't have one of these."
- "Grandpa, you're cool. Thanks!"
- "Oh, wow! Thank you for thinking of me."
- "Red is my favorite color!"
- "This sweater looks nice and warm."

Say it with a smile and a happy tone of voice, and the giver feels appreciated. Most important, teach your child to end by saying thank you. It's nice to make eye contact, too.

Family Activity: Find Something Nice to Say

Fill a laundry basket with various items from around your house, for example, an old sweater, several toys, a mug, a pair of socks. Toss in a few true oddballs, too. Take turns pulling out an item and making a positive comment without exactly saying you like it. You might pull out a pair of purple socks and say, "Hey, I really need socks!" Or grab an outgrown toy and say, "Wow, that's a classic!" or "this looks like fun." Your child gets to practice gracefully accepting any gift, even when it's a bit disappointing. This game is often good for some laughs.

Teach your child to give gifts, too. Even small children can appreciate the good feeling that comes from giving a present. Young children can draw a picture, craft an item, or help bake cookies to give. Older children can put aside some of their allowance or do extra chores to save for buying gifts. Help your kid consider what a particular person might like or use, then choose appropriately.

Be a role model. Keep an ongoing dialogue with your child about both giving and receiving. Share stories about times when giving was especially meaningful to you. And beyond sharing stories, let your actions speak to your child. Always receive gifts with grace and gratitude.

Tip: What Not to Say

When discussing how to accept a gift, it's all about making the gift-giver feel appreciated. Mention to your child what they should *not* say or do:

- Don't put a gift aside without acknowledging it and the giver.
- Don't ask how much an item cost or ask for the receipt.
- Don't say "I don't like it" or "I already have this."
- Don't make fun of the gift or embarrass the giver.

What about the times when a gift seems to be a setup for disappointment? Sometimes gift-givers' judgment is off. Sometimes relatives lose track of kids' shifting interests. Maybe they buy a toy that would be better for a younger child. What do you do?

When Amanda's daughter Sophie was turning six, her mother asked her for some gift suggestions, and Amanda named a few items Sophie had mentioned. At her birthday party, Sophie was thrilled to see her grandmom and couldn't wait to open her presents. But when she unwrapped her grandmom's gift, it was a toy meant for a three-year-old. Disappointed, Sophie looked at her mother. Instead of showing her confusion, her mother nodded, smiled, and said, "What a lovely present." Sophie hesitantly smiled, looked at her grandmother, and said, "I love you, Grandmom. Thank you."

As soon as Amanda saw the present, she knew Sophie would be let down: it was a toy she'd owned as a three-year-old. But before the party, Amanda had coached Sophie on what to do when she opened a gift, no matter what it was:

- Say something nice about the gift.

- Say thank you.

- If the gift is something you don't want, wait until after the party to talk about it.

- Treat all the guests with respect, even if they don't bring a gift, and show them you are glad they are part of your party.

Even three- or four-year-olds can understand not wanting to hurt another person's feelings. They can understand that they should be polite. Be consistent in your expectations, and remind your child beforehand of how to act when given a gift. The bottom line is that people are much more important than things.

Teachable Moment: When the Child Is the Giver

The next time your child gives you a small gift—a drawing, a flower, or a craft from school—tell him how much you appreciate the gift. Let him know you think it's beautiful. Then say something like this: "Hey, let's play pretend, OK? We know I love this gift. But let's pretend I reacted differently. What if I'd said, 'I wish this was a picture of a train, not a car' (or a daisy instead of a dandelion). How would you feel if I'd said that?" Let your child answer, and see where it leads. You might point out that gift-givers have feelings, too. End with reassurance that you do indeed like the gift.

Finish Up with a Thank-You Note

Some people call sending thank-you notes—a handwritten note sent through the postal service—a dying art. While the handwritten note is always appreciated, and a great skill to learn, other modes are fine, too. Your child can send an ecard or email, but each one should be personal, not copied and pasted. For your child, it's one more exercise in verbalizing appreciation.

KEEP CALM AND COACH ON— EVEN WHEN YOUR CHILD'S MANNERS MAKE YOU CRINGE

At your child's last birthday party, maybe they were about as gracious as a wild jackal. Just keep coaching, gently and persistently. Gift-giving—and receiving—is a learned skill. Keep cultivating appreciation and gratitude in small ways: beautiful weather, a beloved pet, a hot meal when we're hungry, a warm bed when we're tired, a funny movie when we need a laugh. Don't save gratitude for only the extras in life. People who practice gratefulness on a daily basis are happier, more optimistic, and physically healthier that those who don't.

Developmentally, children go through phases when they are me-centered, usually as toddlers and again as teens. These times can test your patience, but keep coaching. Even during these phases, your kid is listening. They can keep developing their sense of appreciation for other people—and their enlarged awareness will be more noticeable after the phase passes.

8

Stop Rescuing Your Child

Hector had an important meeting with a client on Thursday afternoon. He planned to drop his son, Jose, at soccer practice on the way to his meeting. Before they left the house, Hector asked Jose to make sure he had everything he needed for practice. "Yeah," Jose said, "I have everything." When they reached the field, Jose opened his sports bag and realized his cleats were missing. "Oh no, Dad, I don't have my cleats. Can you go home and get them and bring them back to me?" Hector knew he'd be late for his appointment, but he didn't want to disappoint Jose. The coach was very strict: players without the proper equipment had to sit on the sidelines and watch everyone else practice. Hector didn't want his son to have to do that. He drove home, found the cleats, and brought them to Jose. He missed the appointment with his client.

• • •

We might think our job as a parent is to make our children happy, to keep them from feeling pain or disappointment. But it's not. Life is full of failures and frustrations. It is through these times that we all learn and grow: children, too. It's how they develop fortitude, self-reliance, and problem-solving skills. When parents swoop in to the rescue, they rob their child of the chance to learn how to manage problems. Success is built upon the lessons we learn through failure.

Is It Really About Your Child—Or Is It About You?

When you step in to save the day, to protect your child from natural consequences—like Jose having to sit on the sidelines—you're not doing them a favor. Jose might feel frustrated and antsy on the bench. Maybe embarrassed, too. But he'd bounce back. He'd learn he can survive a bit of embarrassment: that's valuable knowledge. And don't you think he'll be more likely to remember his cleats next time?

Self-Reflection: What's Your Own Distress Tolerance?

For a parent, seeing your child in pain, whether physical or emotional, is uncomfortable. It hurts. Your whole body aches to take the pain away. If you can intervene, you can make them smile again. But what lesson, what growth might you be depriving them of? Your child can tolerate some discomfort. The question is, can you?

Your job as a parent is to prepare your child for independence. Sometimes loving your child means looking past the present moment to determine what skills they need to develop for the future. What can they learn from the situation that will help them when they are an adult? It may be hard to hold back when your child is three, five, or even fifteen. At this moment, it might not seem like a big deal to give in to the whining and let them have soda with dinner or stay up late. Right now, keeping the peace feels more important than what may or may not happen ten years from now.

Consider This: The Power of Lessons Learned Early

The discomfort young kids feel as a consequence of their mistakes is much less severe than what they might experience later in life. When is it better for a child to learn that bringing homework to school is their responsibility: when they are six or sixteen? At which point is a missing homework assignment likely to have a greater consequence?

But once you give in, it is easier to do so a second, third, or fourth time. Before you know it, your child understands that whining will get them what they want. And, as they grow, what they want isn't as innocuous as staying up an extra half hour. Each time you give in, you ingrain the idea that whining, crying, or pouting works. You are teaching your child how to manipulate and take advantage of people.

Some parents justify their rescuing behavior by defending their "friendship" with their child. They worry that if they say no or set limits that their child isn't going to like them.

Marjorie knew that a good mother-daughter relationship was important during the teen years. Now that Jillian was thirteen, she wanted her to feel free to talk to her about her changing social life, her friends, her anxieties about high school. Marjorie was afraid to strain the relationship—she didn't want to add distance between them. So she found herself catering to Jillian's wants and whims. When Jillian said she was too tired to dust the living room, Marjorie did it instead. When Jillian wanted new jeans, she took her shopping. Being Jillian's "friend" at this crucial time, Marjorie thought, was better than having Jillian angry with her.

Yes, it feels awkward to change the rules. And yes, you might feel like a party pooper when you say no to your child's latest whim. Setting limits can make you feel like the bad cop. But really: you're the *good* cop. Your kid might never admit it, but limits make them feel safe. They'll test them, but if the limits hold, they'll respect them (and on some level, they'll appreciate them). As they grow into their teens, they'll probably push some more—that's age appropriate. But often it's best to hang tough. It hurts when a child shouts "I hate you" or "I wish you weren't my mother" or "you are so mean!" But you'll survive it, and if you don't cave in, you'll win some new respect. Don't let yourself feel taken advantage of, manipulated, and ignored.

What Happens When You Rescue Your Child All the Time?

It's a fact of the human condition: we rarely learn from other people's mistakes. It would certainly be an easier world if we did. No, we learn from our own experience—our successes and especially our failures. And our mixed successes, too: rarely is life black and white. To truly mature, we need to falter, fail, make mistakes, make adjustments, and try again. Through that process we get to know ourselves, and we learn lessons that we carry throughout our lives. But we only learn if we are allowed to falter in the first place.

> At breakfast, nine-year-old Kenji asked his mother to sign his permission slip for an upcoming field trip. Astrid gladly signed it and handed it back, suggesting he put it right into his backpack so he wouldn't forget it. Over the next half hour, she reminded Kenji twice more to put the slip in his pack. Each time, Kenji said he would. But after Kenji got on the bus, Astrid found the permission slip on the floor. She knew it was due that day if Kenji was to join the trip. So on her way to work, Astrid took a detour to drop off the permission slip and then headed to her office, knowing this extra time would make her late.

Consider This: What's Your Unspoken Message?

When you do too much and make all the decisions for your child, you're child may be hearing that you don't have faith in them to make a decision, that you don't believe they are capable, and that you don't trust them to learn from their mistakes.

When you rush in to fix problems, you're denying your child the opportunity to rise to a challenge or admit a mistake. Instead, you're promoting a learned helplessness. When kids are rescued throughout their childhood and teen years, some beliefs and behaviors are likely in later years:

- They avoid taking responsibility for their actions; they might blame others for their mistakes.
- They have trouble identifying and handling uncomfortable emotions.
- They may manipulate others into helping them or finishing their work.
- They act childish when faced with problems.
- They lack self-esteem and self-confidence.
- They often feel that life is unfair.
- They have a negative, fearful outlook.
- They're indecisive and might panic when faced with a major decision.

Whether it's finishing the vacuuming, completing their homework, or confronting a teacher after a bad grade, your kid assumes you'll swoop in. Don't you always? If they never have to dig to find their inner strengths or make hard choices, they might have a hard time keeping a job as an adult. They might seek out a partner who will take over where you left off, or they might resent having to work a job.

As a parent, by the time your child reaches high school you might feel burned out and taken advantage of. You've spent years taking care of someone who shows no appreciation and takes your efforts for granted. Maybe you've neglected your own emotional and physical health as well. You look forward to the day your child leaves home and is off on their own. But hey, if you've been rescuing them all their life, meeting their every need, there's a chance they might not leave. After all, why should they?

When to Help and When to Step Back

A parent's job is to guide and protect. But how do you know if you're doing enough or doing too much? If your child is in danger, being bullied, or in a vulnerable position that requires an adult presence, *you should intervene.* Here are other examples:

- Your toddler runs out into the street.
- Your teen is texting and driving.
- Your teen or young adult is driving drunk.
- Your child is talking to a stranger online.

But most of the decisions your child makes are not going to put them into dangerous situations. These are the times when you can take a step back, let the decision play itself out, and allow your child to deal with the natural consequences:

- Your child doesn't finish their homework.
- Your son wears clothes you don't like.
- Your child gets mad at a friend and decides to end the friendship.
- Your daughter forgets to hand in a permission slip.
- Your teen is late to their part-time job.

These are decisions that have natural consequences. Your child's grades may suffer if they don't hand in his homework, or they might be embarrassed in class. A boss might fire them if they're late too often. Your daughter might miss the field trip. When your child feels sad, upset, or frustrated with the natural consequences, they might choose to do better, work harder, or be on time in the future. If you remove those consequences and rescue your child, they have no reason to change.

And are you doing too much for your child? A good general guideline is that once your child has mastered a skill, it is theirs to do on their own. Once your son has learned to tie his shoes, there's no reason for you to ever do it again. (Thank heaven.) As your child rises to the small challenges of daily life, they're equipping themself for the big challenges up ahead.

Family Activity: "You Can Do It Yourself"

Over the course of a day, notice all the things you do for your child and write them on a list. You might wake your child, lay out clothes, prepare a school lunch, get breakfast, make your child's bed, gather school items, and get your child's coat out of the closet. Continue the list throughout the day. Then review it and put a check next to all the things your child is capable of doing, considering their age and maturity level.

Now choose one or two things you checked and have your child start doing these: packing a lunch and making the bed, for example. Explain that these are now their responsibilities. For a day or two, you might have to remind them. But after that, if they forget, then they must live with the consequence, even if it means going without lunch that day. Keep choosing one or two things at a time to hand over to your child so they learn to take responsibility for themself.

Letting Go

If you are used to doing instead of helping, solving instead of supporting, you might not know where to start to make changes. The following steps offer a guideline to help you get started:

- *Recognize that you're doing too much.* Take off the cape. You've been undermining your child's growth by doing everything and solving every problem.

- *Change your response.* Your child isn't going to become more self-reliant until you decide to stop rescuing. But once you change your reaction—and keep it consistent—they'll change, too.

- *Expect pushback.* Chances are your child won't like having to do things themself, at least not at first. Prepare yourself for crying, whining, and acting helpless. You might even hear, between pitiful sobs, "don't you love me anymore?" Reassure your child you still love them but that they're growing up and can learn to take care of themself.

- *Prepare for your own emotional pain.* Yes, it's hard to let go. You need to deal with feeling helpless for a little while. You'll want to jump in when your child gets frustrated or goes without lunch. Suck it up. It will feel uncomfortable for a bit. Allow yourself to feel these emotions.

- *Be persistent.* Changes don't happen overnight. You are in this for the long term. Be patient and consistent; changes will happen.

▼

KEEP CALM, SUPERPARENT

Admit it: rescuing your child from negative consequences usually makes *you* feel better, right? But if you "cover" for your child when they could have covered for themself, you're probably stunting their growth. And does that feel good, in the long run? So hang up your cape, superhero, and let your child learn the art of self-rescue. In small ways at first, let them see the consequences of their actions and inactions. Then, and only then, will your kid learn to anticipate those outcomes and make choices accordingly. They'll learn to rescue themself by preventing problems and solving them when they do happen. Remember these tips:

- As one version of an old proverb advises: "Give a man a fish and he eats for a day. Teach him to fish and he eats for a lifetime." We're teaching our daughters and sons to fish.

- The next time your child comes to you with a problem and asks what they should do, stop before you offer any ideas. Instead, ask them to write down three possible solutions. Then you can discuss each option to find the one that is best.

- Remind your child often that mistakes are a part of life. We all make them, and we can all learn from them. Let them know that you'll love them no matter the mistakes they make.

9

Why Routines Matter

Think about your everyday family life at home. It's probably structured around daily events such as work hours, school hours, meals, and bedtimes. But in between, you might be scrambling to keep up with other tasks, such as transporting kids to activities, doing household chores, paying bills . . . the list goes on. You never seem to have time to spend together as a family.

It doesn't have to be that way. Let's take a look at how a family schedule, with weekly events and daily routines, can make your life saner—and your child more cooperative.

The Benefits of Routines

How can a daily and weekly schedule help your child become less self-centered? What's the connection? Actually, routines are a real asset for family cooperation and un-entitling:

- *They help dislodge the I-want-it-now mentality,* replacing it with a time-and-place-for-everything mentality. A stable daily routine helps remove an entitled child's wishes from the equation. Want to go to the playground? We do that on Saturdays after lunch. You're hungry? Dinner's at six. Between four and six, you may have a piece of fruit. Want to watch television? You can do so after your homework is done. Routines give your child a sense that there is a predictable order to their life.

- *They help kids become more independent.* With a set time to take a bath, brush teeth, eat breakfast, get ready for school, and complete chores, there are fewer arguments. Your child slowly starts taking responsibility for these tasks themself. You don't need to supervise every task.

- *They help kids develop patience and self-control.* They know they have to wait until a certain time for a particular activity. When your child knows about the playground outing Saturday after lunch, they develop the skills needed to wait for it.

- *They provide a family-based view rather than a self-based view.* Dinnertime is when everyone's home, not when one child is hungry. Everyone in the family follows the daily schedule; it doesn't revolve around just one person's needs.

Consider This: The Health Benefits of Family Mealtime

Children are healthier when they have regular family meals, according to one study. It found that children and adolescents who had family meals at least three times a week were more likely to have a healthy weight, have healthier eating habits, and were less likely to develop disordered eating patterns.[13]

Routines add predictability to your days. When children know what to expect and when, they feel more secure. They're more willing and able to make decisions, take cautious risks, and develop self-confidence and independence. Routines also help to reinforce responsibility. A schedule offers structure, but can also be flexible if called for in an emergency or other unanticipated event.

Creating a Family Schedule

The first step to creating your schedule is to make a list of the main responsibilities and activities for each person. Your list might look like this:

ELIJAH

Work: Monday through Friday, 8 a.m.–4 p.m.
Yoga class: Tuesday evening

JANINE

Work: Tuesday through Saturday, 7 a.m.–3 p.m.
Bowling: Monday and Wednesday evenings

RILEY

School: Monday through Friday, 8 a.m.–3 p.m.
Basketball practice: Monday through Friday, 3 p.m.–5 p.m.
Basketball games: Thursday evening

VERONICA

School: Monday through Friday, 8 a.m.–3 p.m.
Band practice: Monday through Thursday, 3–4:30 p.m.
Clarinet lesson: Tuesday 7 p.m.
Taekwondo class: Saturday morning 10–11:30 a.m.

With the main tasks listed, now you can flesh out a daily schedule for each person, adding in wake-up time, bedtime, meals, and free time. You might want to include assigned tasks: Janine drives Veronica to clarinet lessons; Elijah takes her to taekwondo. You can determine which parent does pickup from after-school activities each day, to help balance responsibilities and eliminate last-minute guesswork. You can plan dinnertime for each night (it might vary), and time when the children should be doing homework. Include chore time and relaxation time—you might call it playtime, social time, exercise time, outdoor time—for each person, too. The idea is to make sure your child has time with friends and is getting fresh air and exercise. (You might make a separate schedule for weekends and holidays.) Let an older child or teen offer some input. If they help plan homework time, computer time, or free time, they're more apt to stick with the schedule.

Tip: The Five-Minute Alert

Especially with a young child, give a heads-up when an activity or event is going to end: "In five minutes, we'll stop playing and eat dinner." Even a child who can't tell time now realizes that a shift in activity is coming soon and can mentally prepare for it. Abrupt endings can be frustrating for children and lead to tantrums.

Adapt your daily routine as your child matures; for example, hours spent on homework will grow over time. And your child will certainly grow more social and independent as they get older. Review your routine at least once a year to make sure it still works for all household members.

There's no ideal to strive for. If a parent works second or third shift, your routine is going to be different from a household with two parents on a nine-to-five schedule. The best routine is the one that works best for your family.

With these individual daily routines set, you can now schedule family time, rather than leaving it to chance. Do the family activity, "What's Important to Each of Us?" Then look over the schedules. You might notice that on Friday evening and

Sundays there isn't much going on, so those could be slated as family time to share meals or other activities.

Family Activity: What's Important to Each of Us?

When setting your schedule, ask all family members to write down one family activity as their top priority. For example, your child might want a weekly family movie night. You might want a midday family meal on Sunday. Incorporating each person's priority helps everyone feel invested in the schedule.

If you find you don't have time for everything, you might have to reconsider your priorities. Are you trying to fit too much into a week? Discuss it as a family.

If you notice that certain times of the day are especially chaotic, such as getting everyone up and out of the house in the morning, write a more detailed schedule for each person—perhaps in the form of a checklist—that includes wake-up time, morning hygiene tasks, getting dressed, breakfast, gathering school items, and so on. This is especially helpful for a young child. A checklist of what needs to be completed helps develop independence. If the chaos persists, review your routine: Are we allotting enough time? Could some tasks be simplified or done the night before? Make adjustments. Feeling chaotic is a sign that the routine needs fixing.

Tip: For a Young Child: A Picture Checklist Schedule

A young child orients themself in their day with events such as mealtimes, playtime, nap time, bedtime. Use these events as anchors for your child's daily routine. Create a picture checklist to help them follow the daily schedule.

Some family timetables are more complex than others: take Raul and Simone's household, for example.

> Raul and Simone worked different shifts. As a hospital nurse, Raul was on duty four twelve-hour days from 2 p.m. until 2 a.m., followed by three days off. Simone worked office hours as a paralegal from nine to five but sometimes later, and sometimes Saturday mornings. Two days a week she worked from home. Raul and Simone had one child in day care and two in elementary school, but with such variable schedules, it was hard to find family time. But once they listed their individual schedules, they discovered they could plan family dinners on Raul's three off days—as long as Simone worked from home at least one of those days, and left at 5 p.m. on the other two. Since neither worked on Sundays, they set Sunday afternoon aside for a family activity and dinner. Rather than planning each day separately, they planned a week at a time, making family time a priority at least several times per week.

Managing Disruptions in the Routine

No matter how well you plan your schedule, it will go off track at times. It might be as simple as your child's sleepover at a friend's, or parents needing to work overtime. It might be planned: overnight camp or vacation. It might be unplanned: an unexpected guest from out of town, a parent who needs care during an illness, the death of a relative. Unexpected and unpredictable events can erode your child's sense of safety and security, and leave them feeling anxious.

Self-Reflection: How Committed Am I to Our Schedule?

If you notice that even with your new routine, your family life still feels haphazard, think about whether you yourself are taking it seriously. Do you see it as more of a guideline than something to strictly follow? Do you think schedules are important for kids, but you aren't so sure you, as an adult, should have to commit to it? The fact is, if you don't commit to the schedule, your child won't either. Don't waste the potential benefits of this surprisingly effective system.

But kids find disruptions more manageable when they occur in the context of a familiar routine. For example, you're working overtime, but your partner makes sure dinner's on the table at six. Or your spouse leaves town because of a family emergency, but you follow your set schedule at home while he's gone. These situations can be learning opportunities: sometimes the unexpected happens, but we'll manage fine as a family. When your child knows that the daily schedule is still the rule and that the regular routine will resume soon (if you can say when, tell them), they are better able to handle emergencies or emotional turmoil. It might help your child to remind them that some parts of the routine remain, such as that they will sleep in their own bed every night, no matter what the day brings. Find what will help your child's sense of security.

▼

KEEP CALM AMIDST THE STORM: YOUR FLUSTER-BUSTER

Whatever the disruption—an emergency trip to see relatives, a family member in the hospital—try to retain some of your daily routine. Even if you feel flustered, your kid will appreciate any stability you can offer. Keep these fluster-buster tips in mind:

- *Provide advance notice if you can.* If you have to work longer hours, let the whole family know what time you'll be home and what changes in the daily routine will occur. In a family emergency, give age-appropriate explanations to let your child know how long you expect the break in routine to last; for example, a death in the family might change the daily schedule for a week or two.

- *Ask your child what's on their mind.* Your child's priorities are different from your own. Ask them what bothers them about the change in situation and address their concerns. (For instance, when one family was planning to move, the young son was worried about whether he would have a closet for his toys in the new house.) Ask, listen, and respond to concerns.

- *Stick to the daily routine as much as possible.* Try to keep meals at the same time and bedtime routines in place. Your child will feel more secure with changes in circumstances if they feel secure with these daily landmarks. If it isn't possible to stick with your daily routine, return to it as soon as possible.

- *Recognize signs of stress in your child.* Stress might show up as whining, irritability, anger, clinginess, crying, insomnia, stomachaches, or headaches. They might become withdrawn. For young kids especially, feelings can be hard to articulate. Be on the lookout for signs of stress and keep in mind that challenging behavior is your child's way of communicating that he can't deal with the current situation.

- *Make time for relaxation.* During times of change, even brief ones, your child might feel stress, much as you do. Plan for fun and relaxing activities, even if the situation doesn't call for it. Make time to go to the playground, have meals together, play a game, or watch a movie together.

- *Teach your child stress-reducing techniques* such as deep breathing, listening to music, or spending time outdoors. Watch to see which strategies work best for your child. Even a young child can be taught to sit quietly and take deep breaths to relax.

Giving your child the skills and emotional fortitude to manage crises in their life helps prepare them for the difficulties of adult life.

10

Kids, Chores, and Money

At some point every family must decide: Should you give your child an allowance—and if so, with what guidelines or restrictions? Should the allowance be tied to chores? Or should you skip the allowance and provide money on an as-needed basis? In this chapter we'll look at the pros and cons of these three options. But no matter which method you choose for your family, the point is to teach your child money management skills so that once they reach the teen and adult years, they've developed good spending and saving habits.

What Are Your Goals?

Before deciding whether, how often, and how much money to give your child, consider what money lessons you most want to accomplish. You can teach all of the following money-related values, but consider which your particular child and family need most:

- *Money management.* As children mature and become adults, they will need to learn how to plan ahead and budget their money in various categories for their savings, gifts, and short- and longer-term needs and wants.

- *Work ethic.* Some parents tie allowances to chores: after all, in the adult world, you receive a paycheck for doing work; if you don't work, you don't get paid.

- *Decision-making skills.* Your child needs practice making wise choices when they can't afford everything they'd like.

- *Giving back.* Some parents make a point of helping those less fortunate. In some families, a part of any allowance is set aside as a donation to a charitable organization.

No matter which way you choose to provide money to your kid, they will benefit from practicing these four values as they grow into adulthood.

Making Allowances

Let's look at the pros and cons of three approaches to providing money to your child: (1) regular allowance, not tied to chores; (2) money provided on an as-needed basis; and (3) allowance as compensation for chores. As you'll see later in this section, each choice can be modified so you'll want to consider possible adaptations before choosing a method. And remember, it's not a permanent decision—you can choose one way of doing it and then evaluate how it's working.

Option 1: Regular Allowance, Not Tied to Chores

Many parents provide their children with a regular and unconditional weekly or monthly allowance, usually at a set time, for example, Saturday morning or the first of the month. The allowance is not tied to any chores or performance. Children receive their allowance because they are part of the family, old enough to need spending money, and their allowance is included in the family budget.

Proponents of this system point out that it can be used to teach money management. With this limited cash, children must prioritize their spending. When the cash is gone, it's gone. But critics believe that an unconditional allowance can raise feelings of entitlement: while parents must work to receive a paycheck, they say, children are handed money simply for existing. It could set kids up for a money-for-nothing mindset. In addition, because there is always more money (next week and the week after that), kids have less reason to budget or save, unless it's for a big-ticket item.

There are several versions of this method. Parents can restrict how allowance is used—for example, clothing only. Some parents buy a prepaid card to a particular store, load it with enough money to buy a season's worth of clothes, and add more money at the start of the next season. In some families, parents insist that a certain percentage be saved, donated to charity, and so on. Parents might also want to think about what conditions, if any, would suspend the allowance. For example, if a child is grounded or otherwise punished, do they still receive the allowance?

Tip: Allowance—How Much Is Enough?

Set your child's allowance at a point where it allows them to strive for a goal and make it, but gives them a chance to make tough choices about what's most important to them. Some families find this a helpful guideline: give between fifty cents and a dollar per year of life, with an increase on each birthday. For example, if you choose fifty cents, your six-year-old would receive three dollars per week.

Option 2: Money Provided on an As-Needed Basis

Plenty of families forego the idea of a set allowance. Instead, children are given money as needed. When a child wants to go the movies, the parent provides the money to buy a ticket and popcorn. When they want to go the mall with friends, they get a certain amount of money to spend. The idea here is that children don't need to get paid for being a member of the family, but that a parent's duty is to provide for their children, and that includes some entertainment.

**Consider This: Teach What Money Can Do—
And What It Can't**

Yes, we can express our values through our money—but money's not the only way we do that. Gifts are a good example. It's kind to buy someone a gift, but even more important is how we treat that person whenever we see them. We show love through actions and words, not just gifts. And while having money can help us buy things to take care of ourselves and others, it cannot buy happiness. Happiness comes from within. Whether we have lots of money or only a little, we can be grateful for what we have. Talk to your child about your attitudes and beliefs about money.

Critics of the as-needed method point to the possibility that children will see their parents as an ATM machine: whenever they want money, it appears. They don't learn the basics of either a work ethic or money management. But this method works fine in conjunction with unpaid chores. Still, parents need to budget realistically for this expense. Many parents who use this method say that their children are very responsible and respectful when asking for money. They say "no," "not right now," or "that isn't in the budget this month" to show that there are limits to how much and how often money is given out. Knowing these limits, kids learn to figure out how much things will cost in advance and ask only for what they need.

When children are taught a sense of responsibility and community at an early age, they are less likely to later demand payment for tasks as they mature. It's not the task and reward that teaches responsibility, it is the conversation, message, and example modeled by the parent that counts.

Option 3: Allowance as Compensation for Chores

Many families choose to tie an allowance to the completion of household chores. This approach often works best with a weekly schedule. Children are given a list of tasks, such as vacuuming, taking out the trash, cleaning the kitchen each night after dinner, mowing the lawn, shoveling snow. (The child's bedroom should not be included in the weekly paid chores. They should be responsible for maintaining their own living space.) Once a week, after parents make sure all the chores have been completed, the children receive their allowance.

Proponents of this method believe that it simulates the adult working world: when you perform a job and do it well, you receive a paycheck. They believe that this type of allowance structure teaches a good work ethic. When you choose not to work, you don't get paid.

Critics claim that household tasks are an important part of a successful family life, and it's everyone's job to help. They believe that paying children for regular household chores sends the wrong message and can lead to entitled thinking—I only need to help around the house if I get paid for it. Other possible problems: If your child doesn't need money one week, they might decide to skip the chores this time. And a kid or teen who picks up outside income—babysitting, a part-time job—might decide that since they don't need your money, good riddance to chores. Would these situations be acceptable to you?

There is a middle ground. You can choose to have two lists of chores: basic tasks and extra tasks. No money is tied to the basic tasks; these are the required weekly chores that all family members are responsible for to keep the household running smoothly. The second set of chores is extras. They might include painting, washing windows, or deep-cleaning the basement. As larger tasks come up, you can add these to the list of extra tasks and set a price you are willing to pay. When your child wants to make money, they can check to see if there are any jobs on this list. The caveat is that that your child's basic household chores must be completed first.

But even this method has its detractors. Suppose you plan to clean and organize the garage this weekend. Your son is watching television and you ask him to help. He automatically wants to know how much money you're offering. Critics say that even the large jobs are part of running a household, and children should learn helping is part of being a family. Still, proponents of this method say that if they're going to give their children money, they would like them to work for it.

A Common-Sense Approach to Choosing Chores for Children

Many parents wonder what chores they should expect their children to do. Of course a lot depends on your particular home and your particular kid. But you might start by looking at some lists on the Internet: enter "age-appropriate chores for children" in your search engine. While these lists are a great starting point, they're somewhat generic. So how do you know what will work for your family?

Family Activity: What Does It Take to
Run the Household?

Your child may have little idea what work gets done behind the scenes at home. They wear clothes that magically appear back in their drawers, clean and folded. They are thirsty and they find drinks in the fridge; they're hungry and dinner appears on the table. Elves and fairies wash the dinner dishes overnight, and they replace that almost-empty toothpaste tube, too.

So, with the entire family together, make a list of every task needed to run your household. Have your child add their ideas to these examples:

- shop for groceries; put items away
- do laundry, including sorting, folding, putting away
- dust surfaces around the house
- sweep and vacuum
- cook meals; wash dishes
- clean kitchen and bathrooms
- do household repairs
- do yard work

Make the list as detailed as possible—it may be eye-opening for your kid. Then talk to them about which tasks they can do, explaining that it takes everyone to keep the household running smoothly and stressing that everyone benefits when everyone works.

Divide the chores according to ability; for example, a younger child probably can't do the wash but should be able to dust or feed the dog. Continue until all the chores on the list have been assigned, as equally as possible based on ability.

A common-sense approach means that each family takes into account their unique lifestyle and home environment. It creates a list of chores for each family member based not only on your home but on the age and abilities of each child. While it is ideal to start this process when your child is a toddler, you can start it anytime you want to incorporate household chores into your child's daily schedule.

Have your child work alongside you when you are doing chores. Instead of using naptime, bedtime, or your child's school day for household tasks, bring your kid into the equation. Set aside specific times when you and your child are home to do chores together:

- Ten minutes before bedtime is a great time to put away toys. At first, have your child work alongside you to pick up the toys, place them in the designated spot, and straighten up. Then try dividing the chore various ways between you: "I'll pick up the blocks; you put the books back on the shelf." Soon you can judge when your child is ready to do the task solo.

- For a young child, find a kid-sized broom. After dinner, have your child sweep a section of the kitchen floor as you sweep the rest. Slowly increase your child's designated area. By the time they're big enough to use a regular broom, they already have the skills to sweep the floor themself.

Tip: Praise Effort

Always remember to praise your child's effort rather than showing disapproval at the end result. Instead of saying "you did that wrong," say "you really tried hard; let's work together to finish." Continued modeling and practice improves the result.

- When setting the table, give your toddler the silverware to bring to the table. As they master that, add the dishes and cups.

You can use the same approach for any household task. Start by working together, and as your child masters the task, you can delegate it to them on a regular basis. This approach takes into account that each child is different. Each has unique emotional and physical development. It also takes into account that you must teach your child how to do chores. It lets you monitor their progress to determine when they are ready to take on a chore by themself.

When you're ready to implement weekly allowances, these tips will be helpful:

- *Designate percentages for spending, saving, and giving.* Set up several containers in your child's room—for example, one for spending, one for saving, and one to donate to a charity of their choice—to divide money into as soon as it is received. The proportions are up to you and should reflect your family's values and spending habits.

- *Decide what spending the allowance should cover.* For a younger child this might include toys, birthday and holiday gifts for family members, and treats when out shopping. For an older child, who receives more money, it might include clothes, transportation, and entertainment. You might agree to continue to pay for shoes, coats, field trips, and other necessities.

- *Discuss the savings portion with your child.* You can designate part of it for long-term savings, such as college or other training. Some could be earmarked for larger items your child wants to purchase: gifts for family members or a combination of the two. Your child gets ongoing practice in delayed gratification as they wait until you can afford an item.

- *Keep a list of banned items and expenditures,* such as electronic devices (until a certain age), tattoos or piercings, pets, violent video games. Giving an allowance to your child does not mean they are free to spend it as they want. Retain veto power even over items that aren't on the list.

Help Kids Learn to Shop Smart

On the other side of the equation, talk with your child about smart spending, too. Plenty of teachable moments here! Give them tips on comparison shopping, teach when to look for long-term value, and at the supermarket call their attention to the unit pricing information on shelf stickers that shows the price per ounce on various package sizes of a product.

Talk to your kid about looking at ads with a skeptical eye. (See chapter 3, "The Entitlement Culture.") Companies spend millions on advertising each year, trying to manipulate our emotions and convince us we need things we don't. They learn our buying profile, so they can target us with the products we're mostly likely to find appealing. Help your child develop an ad-savvy attitude. You might take a don't-be-fooled approach, especially with teens. But be aware—the social pressures to buy can feel strong.

Manuj was looking forward to the weekend, when he was planning to get a new iPhone. He'd seen the commercials, several of his friends already had one, and he was convinced that he "needed" one, too. His father asked, "Why? What can it do that your current phone can't do?" Manuj didn't really have an answer other than that all his friends had one. Although he couldn't explain it, Manuj thought he would be at a disadvantage without the new phone. He thought he wouldn't be as cool as his friends.

For many people, holidays bring buying pressure, too. At Christmas, many feel driven to buy as much as they can, even if it means large credit card bills or deferring other needs. They want to show their children their love by giving them everything they want. A 2015 study found that while almost three-fourths of Americans believed stores should be closed on Thanksgiving Day, more than two-thirds of us do at least some shopping that day.[14]

> Seven-year-old Leah wanted to know whether her family would be going to the mall to "celebrate Black Friday." Her father asked where she'd heard the term *Black Friday*, and she told him about the ads on television. In her mind, it was a holiday celebrated by shopping! Instead of giving in and heading to the mall, Leah's dad took the opportunity to explain how ads try to fool us into buying more than we need and spending more than we should.

When it comes to shopping, it's helpful if your child has earned some money—through babysitting, odd jobs, or in-home chores (if that's your system). That's what shows your child the value of a dollar. If Manuj calculates the value of that new iPhone in hours of mowing neighbors' lawns and raking their leaves, he'll likely treat it with some care. That phone represents a lot of sweat equity.

▼

KEEP CALM: SMALL MISTAKES NOW CAN PREVENT BIG MISTAKES LATER

Money is an area where children can exercise their judgment. Yes, good money habits are important to learn, but here in the kiddie pool, small mistakes can teach good lessons:

- *Let your children make* mistakes when buying items with their own money. For example, your daughter might want to buy a toy even after you indicated it looks cheap and likely to break. So let her discover whatever her decision teaches her. These types of mistakes help your child learn the value of things. Young children can make such mistakes without any real-life consequences, and they may learn valuable lessons.

- *Discuss impulse spending.* Emphasize to your child that spending money is a choice. It's up to them to make wise choices. Remind them that impulsive spending choices often lead to regret later. Suggest they self-impose a twenty-four-hour waiting period before spending their money on an expensive item.

- *Strike a balance* between dictating what your child does with the allowance and giving them free rein. The goal is to teach effective money management. Offer a broad outline of how to manage money and allow your child to fill in the details.

11

Equip Your Child to Make Good Choices

Children are impulsive and spontaneous—that's their nature, especially young kids. And they make impulsive decisions. They don't think in terms of pros and cons, whats and whys, or possible effects on other people. Those are skills that develop gradually through childhood.

As parents, we can help build those skills by offering our kids small, low-risk choices from an early age. We can offer choices that grow in importance, little by little. "Which would you like, a pear or an apple?" "Which shirt will you wear today—the blue one or the red one?" "Which birthday present shall we buy for Lee: this game, or that puzzle?" By the time they're in middle school, they'll be better equipped to consider the consequences of their choices. They've strengthened their decision-making muscles.

Start Early: This One or That One?

Children as young as two or three can make simple decisions, especially when presented with just two options, such as "Which book shall we read—*Winnie-the-Pooh* or *Curious George*?" As three-year-old Juan decides between the blue or purple crayon to color a shirt in his picture, he might think about his own clothes. His favorite shirt is blue, but his mom is wearing purple today: that's a pretty color, too. As five-year-old Zoe contemplates a chocolate, vanilla, or strawberry ice cream cone, she might think about which flavor she had last time, or which one looks especially yummy today. Last time she chose vanilla, but her sister chose chocolate and she wishes she had, too. But she's never tasted strawberry! Maybe she'll try that flavor today. These simple low-risk decisions become practice for bigger decisions.

What to wear, what to eat for breakfast, which game to play? At first, limit the selections to two or three, and keep your questions specific. Avoid open-ended questions, such as "what do you want for a snack?" Instead, frame it as a choice between options: "would you like an apple or an orange for your snack?"

But even with these low-stakes decisions, gently insist that your child live with their choice. If you let them constantly change their mind, you devalue the choice. If the choice doesn't feel real—low stakes though it may be—they won't develop the thinking and imagining skills to make good decisions.

Suppose you ask your four-year-old son, "Do you want a peanut butter and jelly sandwich or grilled cheese for lunch?" He chooses grilled cheese, and you make it. After he eats it, ask if he enjoyed it. If he says yes, congratulate him on making a good decision. If he says he wished he'd chosen peanut butter, point out something good in the outcome—at least he's not hungry anymore—and remind him that he'll get to decide again another day.

As your child matures, you can build up to more options, making decisions a bit more complex, and add in consequences for each choice, such as "we can stay at the playground for another thirty minutes, but if we do, you won't have time to play video games before dinner. Would you rather stay and play with your friends?" Your child learns to judge the pros and cons of a decision.

If your child is indecisive, give a time limit for making a choice. Let them know that if they don't make a decision within that time frame, you'll make it for them.

Five Steps to a Thoughtful Decision

As adults, each of has a personal style and process for making decisions. Some of us might spend time coming up with a long list of potential alternatives. Others might spend time research-ing each option to determine the pros and cons of each. Others use the process of elimination, narrowing down solutions to find the best one. But any way you do it, five basic steps are generally involved:

1. *Identify the decision to be made* (and any parameters in-volved). Frame the question that needs to be answered with a decision: Where shall we go today—to the movies or a ball game? What musical instrument would I like to learn to play? Which makes more sense for me: college or technical school? One common parameter is timing: how quickly must the choice be made?

2. *List the options.* You might do this in your head for small, simple decisions, but for large decisions many people choose to write a list of the choices.

3. *Evaluate the options.* You might spend time researching each alternative, writing down the pros and cons, or discussing the different options with someone. Pace your-self appropriately. For a teen choosing between college

or technical school—and then choosing where to apply within those categories—it may be a months-long process.

4. *Choose.* The moment of truth: make a choice and act on your decision.

5. *Evaluate how it worked.* Once you've implemented your decision (especially a high-stakes one), take the time to evaluate whether it was the right choice. Did it accomplish the given objective? Was it effective? Did it cause harm to anyone? Did it come at too high a cost? Did it resolve problems or cause other ones? If it was a good decision, stick with it. If it wasn't, revise your thinking and change course if possible.

We can even see those five stages unfold as Vince talks his daughter through the simple process of choosing a video.

> Vince and his six-year-old had about an hour to watch a video together. Vince wondered aloud, "What should we watch? There are a few good movies, but we don't have much time, so let's look for a shorter program. You really liked the show we saw the other day, *Doc McStuffins*, right? But we haven't seen *Wild Kratts* in a long time. Let's watch that! It's about animals, and we both love animals." Later, they agreed that *Wild Kratts* was one of their favorite shows ever.

As Vince talked through his reasoning, he was demonstrating decision-making in action. You can do the same as you make daily decisions in your child's presence: what to make for dinner, what route to take to do errands, what book to choose at the library. For some decisions, you can stop and ask your child what choice they would make and then ask them to explain why.

Later On: Child-Initiated Choices

As children mature and start having their own ideas they'd like to act on, decisions become more complex and the potential stakes higher. And especially if the idea means mischief, they probably won't consult with you. So, to help lower the odds of rash decisions later, establish a habit of self-questioning when your child is still young. Teach your child to ask themself a few questions before deciding whether to act on an idea:

- Why do I want to do this?
- What are my options?
- What are the consequences? What might happen to me, and to others, if I do this?
- Is this the right decision?

In the beginning, simply ask your child these questions—don't answer, just ask—and listen to what they say. As you guide your daughter through these questions for her own simple daily decisions, she'll get into the habit of using them. It might seem silly to ask a young child these questions about the simple idea of going to the pool to swim on a hot day. But the point is to make the questions reflexive. Soon enough, her decisions really will matter. As a teen, face it: your daughter might be with

---

Tip: Keep Your Right to Veto

There are times when a parent needs to veto a decision. As you begin letting your child make more choices, let them know that you have the final say. If your child's choice might lead to a dangerous situation or could harm another person physically or emotionally, step in to guide your child to making a better decision. If your child is insistent, you might need to veto the decision.

Family Activity: What Would You Do?

When reading a story aloud together, look for moments when a character has to make a decision. Stop reading before the character makes the choice and say, "Let's stop for a minute and pretend. What would you do if you were that character?" Listen, and encourage your child to explain their choice. You can also share your ideas, but without disagreeing with or criticizing your child's decision. With this activity, you're considering options and forming opinions; it's not about making the "right" decision. Hear your child out, then keep reading aloud. When the story is over, there might be more to talk about as you reflect on the outcome of the character's choice.

---

peers who are considering shoplifting, using drugs, drinking, or skipping school. If this question habit is ingrained, it could help her make the right choice. At the very least, even if she makes a bad choice, she'll probably feel more accountable afterward.

You're installing a rudimentary risk-and-reward gauge in your child's brain. In these tempting situations, kids often underestimate the costs. They think no one will ever know. And even if they do know, they won't get in trouble. And even if they do get caught, the punishment won't be too bad. They also overestimate the benefits: this will be so much fun it will be worth a little punishment. These questions can help them step back and take a more realistic look.

Using Values to Guide Decisions

Each of us has a set of personal values that guide our choices. Your values might not be the same as your partner's, neighbor's, sister's, or child's. Often our values are fairly stable throughout our lives, but they can change along with our circumstances. A young, single career person might value money and status highly, but a person who has a job and family might see work/life balance as most important.

What qualities about your child do you value? What do you think your child most values about themself? Although younger children don't always have the words to describe their values, they still have some idea of what is important to them. As they grow up, children can become aware of the kind of person they want to be. Some examples include generous, hardworking, cheerful, caring, creative, dependable, truthful, good at listening, and good at being a friend.

As our children make decisions, they will consider these values even before they realize they're doing so. As they mature, they're better equipped to understand and verbalize how they see themselves and what type of person they want to be. Once your child is in middle school or high school, you can help them

---

Tip: Be a Decision-Making Coach

At some point, your child will come to you and ask what they should do about some situation or other. Rather than tell them what to do, help them come to their own decision:

- "That does sound like a hard decision. What are you thinking?"
- "Can you tell me three ways you could handle this? Which one are you leaning toward?"

End with "I have a lot of faith in you; I know you will be able to figure this out," or "you are a good problem-solver, I am sure you will make the right decision," or "I trust you to make the best decision you can; and if it turns out to be wrong, I trust you will learn from it."

---

identify their strongest values and remind them that before making a decision, they can measure it against their values. If they don't match, they might want to reconsider that choice.

Holding Children Accountable for Their Decisions

Every decision has a consequence. Some of these are neutral, for example, choosing to color with the purple crayon instead of the blue one. Some are minor; for example, choosing not to eat dinner might result in being hungry later. But as your child matures, decisions come with bigger consequences. Not studying for a test means a lower grade. In younger grades and middle school, this might simply be disappointing, or it might

---

Family Activity: What If...?

Make up hypothetical situations and have each person take a turn talking about what they would do. Encourage your child to think about whether their actions fit with their values:

- You are invited to two birthday parties that are at the same time on the same day. Which one do you attend?
- You see someone being bullied. What do you do? Would it make a difference if you were friends with the person or if you didn't know the person who was being bullied?
- You win a $100. How will you spend it?
- You find a ten-dollar bill on the sidewalk. What will you do?
- You said something that hurt another person's feelings even though that wasn't your intention. What do you do?

During the game, discuss looking at situations from other people's perspectives. Does that change your reactions? Ask questions to dig deeper into the decision-making process used and the values that guide it.

---

lead to loss of a certain privilege at home. In high school, it could result in not getting into the college of your choice.

When you don't hold your child accountable for their decisions at a young age, they grow up believing that they should get whatever they want, no matter whether they made a good decision or not. As adults, they might have trouble accepting responsibility for a mistake: "It's your fault the cable was turned off; you didn't remind me to pay the bill."

There are times it would be easier to give in and let your child reverse a decision, but think twice before you do. For example, your son might ask if he can take a six-week art class on Tuesdays this summer. You sign him up and take him to two classes, but he decides he doesn't like it. It might be easier to let him quit—after all, who wants to listen to him whine every Tuesday for another month? But that would send the message that he isn't responsible for sticking to a decision. Instead, tell your son that he made a commitment and must complete the classes. At that point, it's okay if he decides he doesn't want to sign up for another session.

Let's consider a few more examples:

- Your daughter receives twenty dollars for her birthday. She chooses a toy at the store, but when you get home, she changes her mind and wants to exchange it for a different toy.

- Your child asks for French toast for breakfast. After you prepare the egg batter, they change their mind and ask for scrambled eggs.

- Your son wants to wear the shirt with the dinosaur on it. When he gets to school and sees his friend in a superhero shirt, he wants to go home and change his shirt to match his friend's.

In each of these situations, you could give in—you could go back to the store and exchange the toy, throw away the French toast batter and make scrambled eggs, take your child home to change. Or you can teach your child the lesson that we aren't always happy with our decisions, but that's okay. We're still fine, and we'll have another chance to choose next time.

Teachable Moment: Why'd I Do That?

We all make poor decisions sometimes: it's part of learning how to make good ones. After your child makes a poor choice, see if there's a good chance to talk about it, maybe after a bit of time has passed. Ask gently what might have prompted that choice. There are many common reasons they might offer:

- didn't stop to think about the consequences
- seemed fun at the time
- boredom
- peer pressure
- pressure to make a quick decision
- anger, spite, or vengeance

Making poor decisions is a necessary part of childhood. If you can't pinpoint the reason for the poor decision, you might be more apt to make it again.

When you teach your child that decisions have consequences they'll have to live with, they'll put more thought into their choices. That's especially important as your child matures. Teenagers have more consequential decisions: Shall I try drugs just because my friends are doing them? Should I bother studying for this test? If they've practiced good decision-making processes, they'll look at their choices more carefully.

Keep in mind, however, that parents should veto any decisions that go against their morals or put any child's safety at risk.

KEEP CALM, EVEN WHEN TRIAL AND ERROR FEELS TRYING

Our lives are full of trial and error. Your child is bound to make some poor decisions, just as you have (and probably still do). Don't panic. If you've modeled good decision-making, and if you teach the skills in this chapter, your child will be gaining the resilience to learn a lesson and choose better next time. Here are a few reminders from the chapter:

- *Limit choices for younger children.* Too many options can be overwhelming. As your child gets older, expand both the number of chances to make a decision and the number of options to choose from.

- *Reflect briefly on decisions afterward.* After a satisfying decision, remind your child what was good about it. If your child is not satisfied with a decision, discuss what they could have done differently.

- *Attitudes and behaviors are choices, too.* Sometimes a decision is an adult's to make—such as when it's time to go home. Your child might feel sad, but remind them that they can choose an attitude, such as "let's be grateful for that hour at the playground" or "let's plan another fun time with friends."

- *Help your child reframe blame.* When you hear your child blaming others when things don't go their way, help them

— continued —

reframe their thoughts and accept responsibility. If your daughter doesn't score a goal during a soccer game and blames her teammates for not covering her, you can help her reframe: "if I practice more, I will improve my playing" or even "how can I cover other players better, so we all feel more supported?"

12

Dealing with Feelings

In the drugstore checkout line, Anika's four-year-old daughter noticed a stuffed bear on display. Darsha's eyes lit up. "Mommy, look at that bear! Can we bring it home? Please?" she asked. "No, honey," said Anika, "we're not going to get the bear." Darsha's face fell. She stayed quiet, but her lips quivered and tears welled up in her eyes. As Anika paid for her purchases, Darsha started to cry silently. Anika felt terrible. Darsha was suffering! No decent mother would let her child heave with sobs this way! Anika bought the bear.

• • •

Children, like adults, have a wide range of emotions. They feel joy, fear, anxiety, pride, worry, giddiness, and love. Sometimes they feel sad or disappointed. These are all normal feelings, and your child has a lifetime of them ahead. The negative feelings are as much a part of the human condition as the positive ones. (Have you noticed?) So we'd better learn to live with them. Feelings help us understand ourselves better, and if we manage them well, they can help us make good choices. When we pre-empt our kids' uncomfortable feelings, we rob them of the chance to manage those feelings and bounce back from them. And isn't that a skill they're going to need?

Don't Let Your Child's Emotions Control Yours

You might recognize yourself in Anika. The setting might be different, but you've had moments when you've given in to your child's impulsive request because they're disappointed, frustrated, or irritable. You worry that when your child isn't happy, you must have done something wrong.

News flash: life has ups and downs. Some days are good, some are bad; many are mixed. Each day we navigate myriad emotions of our own. In the morning, we might feel proud when everyone gets out of the house on time. Then we feel irritated while stuck in traffic on our way to work. We're disappointed when our performance review is so-so; back at our desk we worry about a relative's health; we're hurt when a colleague cancels lunch plans. Once home, we might be annoyed at our partner for forgetting to pick up dinner and upset when our child leaves an assignment at school. Despite all the emotions we felt through the day, once we sit down to relax, we might feel contentment and love for our family. We're managing our emotions; they're not managing us.

Remember, our job as a parent isn't to protect our child from unpleasant feelings. Our job is to help them develop the skills they'll need to manage all the feelings they'll have throughout their own wonderful, challenging, happy, sad, crazy, glorious life. If Anika buys the bear, yes, it might make Darsha smile.

Self-Reflection: Children Feel What We Feel

No doubt, our kids pick up our vibes. For children, parents are an anchor. So if we feel distressed, our child might feel edgy or insecure. When your child seems moody, ask yourself if they're reflecting your own feelings. If so, see if you can manage those emotions a bit more consciously.

But it's a temporary fix. If Darsha doesn't get to feel sad and let down, she won't learn that she can bounce back from sadness. She'll have less emotional experience to draw on in her future.

With young children, feelings often pass quickly. Changing the subject or offering a distraction can do the trick. ("Robbie, it's time to catch the bus home. Let's go see who's waiting at the stop!") With older kids, feelings and moods can linger longer. And when we're setting limits on what our children can do, we can expect pushback. If feelings run high, it's generally best to meet your child's strong emotions with calm. When high emotion meets high emotion, the situation tends to escalate.

Jericho's thirteen-year-old daughter, Kim, wanted to go to a party on Friday night. It was her first "real" party, in the evening, with girls and boys, and she was excited. Jericho wanted to know more: who's hosting it, the address, the time frame, the parents' phone number. He told Kim that until he spoke with at least one adult who would be at the party he was withholding his permission. "Dad! Everyone's going! Don't you trust me?" Kim asked, her voice rising. "I know all these kids! It's fine!" She stormed into her room, slamming the door behind her. Jericho followed Kim into her room, scolding his daughter. The fight escalated into a shouting match. Jericho told Kim she couldn't go to the party.

Jericho met his daughter's high emotion with his own, and both ended up disappointed and upset. Had Jericho remained calm, the conversation might have gone differently:

Kim: Dad, I'm invited to a party Friday night! Can I go?

Jericho: You seem excited about it! Who's giving the party?

Kim: Debra. She's in my class.

Jericho: And what time does it start and end?

Kim: It starts at 7.

Jericho: Well, I'll need a little more information first. Could you give me Debra's address and her parents' phone number, please? I'd like to call to make sure an adult will be at home. And I'd like to check on the ending time, too.

Kim: I have the address written down, and Debra said her parents would be home. You don't need to call! It makes me feel like a baby. You should trust me!

Jericho: I understand you don't want me to call. I do trust you, Kim, but this is a new situation for you, and we don't know exactly what to expect. It's your first evening party, and I'm a little nervous. I haven't met Debra's parents yet. I'll feel more comfortable if I speak with her mom or dad before the party.

Kim: This isn't fair!

Jericho: I understand it's frustrating, but I still need the number.

In this example, Jericho stayed calm during the conversation, despite Kim's being upset, then went back to his chores. A few minutes later Kim returned. She was disgruntled, but she gave the phone number and address to her dad.

When you model healthy management of your own feelings, your child learns to handle their emotions in the same way. When you speak sharply or shout, so will they. When you speak respectfully, they learn to do the same.

Emotions: Showing, Then Telling

Young children often wear their emotions on their face. With a glance, you can tell if your son is frustrated, proud, or happy.

You can read it long before he learns to articulate it. When that emotion looks like trouble—anger, say—our first instinct might be to try to neutralize it, to bring the child back to a happy state. And let's admit it, sometimes we're just trying to prevent the *behavior* that might accompany the anger: crying, sulking, yelling, hitting, kicking, whining, pouting.

Young kids act out their emotions. They don't know the words to describe how they're feeling. They aren't able to say, "I'm disappointed, Mommy—I wanted that toy." When your six-year-old son has trouble finishing a puzzle, he might growl or yell instead of saying, "I'm frustrated!" When your daughter's block tower falls, she might stomp her feet instead of saying, "I'm upset! I put a lot of work into that!" Your child isn't trying to hurt you or annoy you—they're just expressing feelings the only way they know how.

But we can start heading off that behavior by talking with our kids about their feelings, helping them start to recognize them. With small children, it's often smart to go to their level—literally. Kneel on the floor or sit at their level so you can see eye to eye. It sets a tone of safety and openness, and you'll both read each other's faces better. For toddlers, you can make an "emoji board," showing faces wearing a variety of expressions. Your child can choose the face that fits how they're feeling. Over time, learning lots of "feeling words" will help any child communicate better.

The Language of Feelings

As an adult, you've gained an extensive vocabulary to describe emotions. But kids are at the beginning of that learning curve. And there's a big range to learn. It takes a while; even teenagers can have trouble pinpointing their feelings (and under stress, so can adults, right?). So, in age-appropriate ways, help your kid learn the wide span of emotions and how to name them:

- *Name your own feelings when talking to your child.* "Where are my keys? I'm confused. I thought they were in my pocket." "That's so annoying! The cat got outside again." "I'm disappointed it's raining—we'll have to postpone our picnic." Just as you can read your child's face, she can read yours. She knows your facial expressions, and as you give each one a name, she begins to internalize what confused, annoyed, and disappointed look like.

- *Guess at and name your child's feelings.* Before you react, name how you believe they are feeling: "It seems like maybe you're angry—are you?" "You look excited this morning!" "Are your feelings hurt?"

- *Point out what others seem to be feeling.* When reading a book or watching a television show, you might say, "She seems exhausted, doesn't she?" or "He looks surprised by that big package on the porch!" or "She looks worried about her dog."

- *Use a variety of emotion words* to help your child discern a range of feelings:
  - *angry:* annoyed, disgusted, furious, mad, outraged, upset
  - *confident:* capable, eager, optimistic, sure, strong
  - *embarrassed:* foolish, guilty, mortified, regretful, shameful
  - *happy:* cheerful, delighted, ecstatic, excited, joyful
  - *hurt:* belittled, cheated, disappointed, dismayed
  - *loving:* affectionate, caring, devoted

- *sad:* depressed, miserable, unhappy, melancholy
- *satisfied:* content, pleased, peaceful
- *scared:* afraid, fearful, frightened, nervous, terrified
- *surprised:* amazed, astonished, shocked
- *thankful:* appreciative, grateful
- *uncertain:* doubtful, suspicious, unsure, distrustful, wary
- *worried:* anxious, bothered, scared, tense, agitated

As you continue to name feelings as they come up, your child will get better at describing how they feel.

Family Activity: Emotion Charades

Recognizing how other people feel is a skill, too. Try this game when the family's together. Beforehand, using slips of paper or index cards, write down one emotion on each. Make it a wide range of strong feelings, from shocked to thrilled to scared. Have family members take turns choosing a card and acting out that feeling—without using words. Other family members guess the emotion.

As you talk about unpleasant feelings, you might help your child identify three strategies to deal with each one. For example, you might say, "When I'm sad, I can take a walk, listen to music, or talk to someone. When I'm frustrated, I can take a break from what I'm doing, ask for help, or take several deep breaths and try again."

Use role-playing to help your child handle feelings in inter-actions with others. Suggest a few challenging situations and role-play a dialogue together. For example, what if a classmate made fun of your child, or accused them of cheating on a test?

What if they had a fight with their best friend or lost a cherished possession? If you and your child take turns playing the different roles, your child will learn to look at situations from different perspectives as well as gaining ideas on how to handle these difficult moments.

How We Feel and How We Behave: An Important Difference

All emotions are real, and all emotions are acceptable. But not all *behaviors* are. Your child is entitled to feel whatever emotion they feel. If they are angry, telling them they shouldn't be angry doesn't mean the anger disappears. Emotions are a normal human reaction to what is going on around us.

Tip: Don't Assume

You shouldn't assume you know how your child feels because you know how you would feel in a situation. Just as some people like vanilla, or chocolate, or macadamia caramel ripple ice cream, people can have different emotions in reaction to the same situation. Use words like "you seem angry" or "it looks like you are feeling scared" rather than telling your child how they feel.

When we're feeling strong emotions, we often feel impulses, too—both good and bad. Impulses, like emotions, are not wrong. When angry, we might *feel* the impulse to hit someone or use hurtful names, but it's not acceptable to *act* on that impulse. Other impulses might be more debatable. If we feel happy, we might have an impulse to hug someone. This might be appropriate if it is a family member, but it might not be appropriate to hug a stranger. This is a difficult concept for your child to understand. Teaching them acceptable ways to manage their emotions includes teaching them when and how to act on the impulses that come with those emotions. We can't choose how we feel, but we *can* choose how we behave and how we express the way we feel.

▼

KEEP CALM ON THE ROLLER COASTER OF FEELINGS

Help your child manage feelings as they come up. These basic steps work at any age:

- *Name and validate the feelings.* Empathize with your child. Suggest emotions they might be feeling, for example, "You seem angry. Or are you worried? Let's talk about it." Show that you understand. Keep calm while you're discussing it. Your raised emotions can escalate the situation.

- *Deal with behaviors.* If your child has acted inappropriately out of anger, deal with the behavior immediately. If they have hurt someone or damaged property, hold them accountable. Use a time out, have them apologize to the person, and discuss how they will replace the damaged property. Remind them that while the emotion is understandable, the behavior was not acceptable.

- *Discuss what caused the emotion.* Once your child is calm, talk about what happened. Discuss the situation leading up to the intense emotions. Name the other emotions that your child might have been feeling, such as saying, "I can see why you got angry. This sounds like it was frustrating." This helps your child understand how one emotion, when not dealt with, can lead to a stronger emotion. Encourage your child to talk about how they felt; let them know that while behaviors can be wrong, it is never wrong to talk about feelings.

- *Find strategies for dealing with this emotion.* Talk about techniques your child can use when feeling overwhelmed:
    - take three deep breaths
    - count to ten
    - talk to someone about how you feel
    - ask for help
    - do something active, such as ride a bike, run around outside, or dance
    - listen to music
    - write down your feelings
    - use self-talk ("I can handle this"; "I'm frustrated so I'll take a ten-minute break to calm down.")

The goal is not to avoid the strong emotions, but to find ways to manage them before they escalate. You're coaching your child, but in the long run, your child is developing lifelong skills for self-managing emotions.

13

Why Words Matter

KINDNESS IN ACTION

When do you feel most proud of your child? When they get a scout badge or an A on a math test? When they score the winning basket or play *Für Elise* flawlessly during the piano recital? Or do you feel most proud when you see your child being kind and caring to someone—perhaps a younger child or an elderly relative?

If kindness makes you proudest, most kids would be surprised. In one national study, about 80 percent of the youth surveyed believed that their parents were more concerned with their achievements than whether they were kind to others.[15] But in a different study, most parents said that raising kind children was a top priority.[16]

Somehow, what parents say they value isn't coming across to their children. When our child shows kindness, maybe we overlook it because we expect it, especially if we model it ourselves. When a neighbor is away, we get their mail and feed their cats. When a coworker's car is in the shop, we drive them home. We believe that we are being kind, and we expect our children to act the same.

Or maybe we're not especially good role models. In fact, we may spend most of our time taking care of our own needs, and frankly, we're self-involved in our own world. We don't mean to shut others out; we simply focus on our daily life and don't have much left—financially, emotionally, or timewise—to take care of others.

Young children often help others because it helps them get what they want—attention or maybe a small treat. As they get older, they might do so because they get praise. But as children start school and other activities, do you give praise more freely for success than for acts of kindness? Yes, probably. It's a natural progression, but one that could imply to kids that personal achievements are more important than kindness.

Consider This: Kindness Does Not Equal Weakness

Will teaching your child kindness make them a pushover? No. Often, real kindness requires assertiveness, too. We learn to view a situation from another person's perspective; for example, how would they feel if they were the new person joining class in January? And then it means acting on that insight: talk with the new student, invite them to join a game, introduce them to friends. That's both kind *and* assertive.

Teaching Kindness: Habits to Cultivate

Make time as a family to reach out to others. If you hear of a family in your neighborhood that is having a hard time, through job loss or other misfortune, what could you do together to help? You could invite them to a pizza and movie night at your place. Maybe you can gather household goods from friends and neighbors if someone's home has been damaged. Maybe you can cook a few meals, do yard work, or run errands for someone who's had a death in the family. As you reach out to others, and include your child, they'll see this as the right way to act:

- *Praise your child's kindness toward others.* Look for small ways your child helps others, such as picking up an item someone dropped at the store, holding the door for someone, or helping an elderly neighbor carry groceries into the house. Whenever you notice your child doing a kindness, make sure to acknowledge it.

- *Model everyday kindness, in word and deed.* Always show kindness when talking with cashiers at the store, customer service reps on the phone, people you pass by each day. Say hello with a smile and treat them as you'd like to be treated. Your child will pick up the habit.

- *When you see an opportunity to be kind, take it.* If you see someone who needs help, offer your assistance. Give a hand to another child at the playground. If you know a friend isn't feeling well, reach out to see if they need anything. There are endless opportunities every day to be kind to someone else.

- *Point out the goodness of others.* Watching the news can make anyone believe that there is a lot of evil in this world. But many acts of kindness happen each day—we just don't hear about or focus on them. Look for stories of people helping others, in both big and small ways, to show your child there's a great deal of good in the world.

Teach Children That Words Matter

"Sticks and stones may break my bones, but words will never harm me." Let's face it—this old proverb is wishful thinking. Anyone who's been at the receiving end of cruel words knows that it's just not true. Cruel words can hurt deeply; some scars can last a lifetime. And once unkind words have been said, they can't be taken back. Another person's words can make us feel put down, ridiculed, dismissed, or unwelcome. Another person's choice *not* to speak to us can even make us feel invisible.

On the other hand, kind words can also last a lifetime. Sincere words of welcome, appreciation, thanks, admiration, an offer of help—these lift us up. Another's kindness when we feel down or vulnerable can have long-lasting effects. Not only that, but kind words make the giver feel good, too.

Family Activity: Words Stay With Us

Think back to a time when you were given a compliment. "Hey, great presentation at the meeting!" "You're an amazing woodworker/cook/car mechanic." "How'd you get so good at basketball?" Or maybe just "love the haircut!" You probably felt good inside, maybe held your head a little higher, maybe felt inspired to be more pleasant to others. You might still remember a compliment you received years ago.

Now think about a time when someone said something unkind. Maybe a coworker slighted you, or your significant other was sarcastic, or a sibling lashed out at you. You probably felt defensive, hurt, and upset; maybe you lashed out at someone else afterward.

When your family's together—say, at the dinner table— have each person tell about a time when someone's words, kind or unkind, really stuck with them. What effects did those words have? Words stay with us, and they often have ripple effects.

If we're kind to others, we're more likely to be treated with kindness. If we easily show unkindness, hostility, or impatience, we could be treated with the same. Kindness can take effort. Like gratitude, kindness is a skill. And, like gratitude, if we cultivate kindness—the younger the better—it becomes second nature.

Sticks and Stones May Break My Bones, but Social Media Lasts Forever

Social networks offer children a way to expand their circle of contacts. In many ways they offer great opportunity: your child can see how other people live. They can friend someone in another nation and hear about the struggles and joys of living in a different culture. Social networks can give you and your child a sense of being connected to others and can deepen friendships.

But there's a dark side, too. They offer a sense of anonymity; some people feel empowered to say things they wouldn't normally feel comfortable saying. When someone is standing right in front of you, you might not consider insulting him. But online, children and teens can forget that there is a real person, with real feelings, behind the profile. According to a 2016 study from the Cyberbullying Research Center, 33.8 percent of students report being cyberbullied at some time.[17] Cyberbullying includes many behaviors:

- posting mean, hurtful, abusive, or threatening messages on social networks
- stealing a person's login information, then posting content that could damage the person's reputation or turn others against them
- posting unflattering or sexually suggestive pictures of someone
- engaging in aggressive conversations, called "flaming"
- sharing someone's secrets in an effort to embarrass them

Online, people are more likely to be mocked for physical features such as weight, and to be the target of bigoted remarks about their race, ethnicity, or religion. Because social networks are so broad, some people who join in the conversation can easily belittle you without ever having met you.

Consider This: Likes Do Not Equal Validation

For some, gaining likes and shares for a post, photo, or video becomes a craving of sorts. But these forms of cyber validation are hollow; the ego boost they offer is momentary and fosters a dependency on outward validation.

Embarrassing moments have the potential to become truly humiliating when they are shared online and everyone at school (and around the world) has the chance to laugh about it. Remember those trivial but mortifying high-school moments? You leave the bathroom dragging toilet paper from your shoe, and the kids in the hallway tease you. You confide in a friend—"I really like that new guy, Derek!"—and Derek hears you and says, "Forget it." Imagine someone caught it on video and shared it online. Now imagine the snickers as it goes viral among your "friends."

This doesn't just happen in social networks. People who play online games frequently report being bullied or witnessing someone else being bullied. One reason is that people of various maturity and skill levels often play together. Some people take their online gaming very seriously; they mock, abuse, or threaten other players when the game doesn't go well. Players who have an accent or ethnic name might be harassed, too.

Riot Games, the maker of the popular online game League of Legends, has taken steps to curb the online bullying. They have a system for reporting abusive or offensive players. They may suspend or ban players who continue to mistreat others. Users can also mute individual players if they wish.

With online activity increasing, our formerly private lives are laid out for public consumption. And with that comes the potential for public ridicule, shame, and criticism. An adult who chooses a life in the public eye might be prepared to handle these consequences. But your typical fourteen-year-old doesn't make that choice or understand that they're making that choice.

Words matter. Words have the capacity to lift us up or tear us down. Besides being kind to the people we see and meet, it is important to be kind online. Parents can help reduce cyberbullying and other forms of online harassment by taking these steps:

- *Talk to your child or teen about cyberbullying,* explaining that the same rules for in-person kindness apply online as well.

- *Make a household rule to do no harm.* No one may send mean, damaging, or threatening messages to another person or comment on such messages posted by others.

- *Remind your child the Internet is public.* They should not post, text, or email any message that they wouldn't want posted on a billboard on the highway for everyone to see. Anything sent electronically has the potential to be seen by masses of people. And it can have a long life even if the originator deletes it. If someone took a screenshot, shared it, or forwarded it, we can't erase it.

- *Emphasize keeping passwords safe.* Teens should never tell their friends their password.

- *Encourage your child to report incidents* of cyberbullying they witness online, whether it happens to them or someone else. Have them take screen shots of the posts so you can talk to the appropriate people, such as the parents of the targeted person.

- *Reassure your child* that if they are the target of cyber-bullying, they are not at fault and will not be punished. Some children hesitate to tell parents because they are afraid they will lose their Internet access or use of their cell phone.

- *Think of the future.* Let teens know that negative comments, meanness, bullying, and inappropriate posts can damage their future prospects for college and job opportunities. Online posts can follow them for years.

Remind your child or teen that behind each profile is a real person with real feelings. Everyone, both in-person and online, should be treated with respect and courtesy.

KEEP CALM ON THE SLIPPERY SLOPE THAT STARTS WITH TEASING

Do you sometimes overhear your kid teasing their friends? Listen carefully: Is it good-natured, or is there an edge? How does the recipient handle it? Help your child understand the differences between teasing, harassing, and bullying. Friends and family members often tease one another. They say disparaging things in a humorous way, and often that's just fine. But there's a thin line between teasing and harassment, and it hinges both on how it is delivered *and* how it is received. Teasing is only appropriate between people who know each other well and only in an affectionate spirit. Even so, the other person may be upset or hurt. A general rule of thumb is that if the receiver doesn't see it as funny, it *isn't* funny, an apology should be issued, and no further teasing should occur.

Share stories about children who experienced teasing. Look for books, movies, or online blogs that share how it felt to be teased or harassed, and how it affected the lives of those on the receiving end. Putting a face and voice to the pain of being teased or harassed might help your child view it differently.

When watching a television program, movie, or video, be quick to point out when either a kind or unkind comment is made. Have your child reflect on what makes it kind (or unkind); this is especially useful when you can pause the action to discuss, and then resume. It may also help children identify sarcasm and the importance of tone of voice—a tone that is often lost or misinterpreted in online posts.

14

Give Back

One December day, Marilyn and her three children went shopping for holiday gifts, but not for relatives and friends. Each child picked out two presents to donate to a family in need. It was a family tradition from Marilyn's own childhood. Marilyn wanted to teach her children that the holidays are a time to spread goodwill. But she didn't want her children to think that the holidays were the *only* time to give, either. So once each season—spring, summer, fall, and winter—Marilyn found some way for her family to give back to her community. Once her children collected sheets, towels, and clothes for a local family whose house had burned down. During the summer, the family set out for the park early Sunday mornings to pick up litter. When they heard about a natural disaster, they donated money to help the survivors rebuild. Marilyn believed that it was important to share their good fortune with others.

• • •

Let's Move Outside Our Bubble

Sometimes our lives feel like a never-ending chase. It's easy to get consumed with buying more or wanting the newest gadget, the extravagant vacation, the latest car. Our thoughts can help us develop an I-deserve-it attitude:

- I work hard. I deserve to spend my money and buy myself something special.
- I had a terrible week; I need a treat.
- I got a promotion; this is my reward.
- I sacrificed for my child, now I deserve to get whatever I want.
- My boss was mean to me; I deserve to do something nice for myself.
- I am under so much stress, buying this will make me feel better.

We come up with excuse after excuse to buy and collect more things. These attitudes are passed on to our children, often without us even realizing it. When our lives become about us and our families, exclusively, we create a bubble and our children live comfortably inside it with us. We live as if we don't need anyone outside of our bubble, and therefore, the people outside it don't need anything from us.

But that's not true. Each person is part of a family, community, city, or town. We are part of a state, part of a country, part of the world. We are all connected, and we all need one another. The world, and everyone in it, is much better off when everyone contributes to their family, their community, and the world in general.

Teachable Moment: When Misfortune Strikes Others

Select one recent story from the news about a natural disaster somewhere in the world: a tornado, flood, or earthquake, for example. Then discuss that event with your child: what happened, and how did it affect that community? (You might find out more from the Internet.) As a family, you might decide to donate money or goods, if appropriate. Children learn that when disasters happen, other people (including them) can provide help and support.

Obstacles to Giving Back

What stops you from giving back? Are you too tired? Too busy? Maybe you're in debt, barely paying your own bills. Do any of the following reasons sound familiar?

- You're saving for family needs, your child's college funds, a new house, or other personal expenses.
- You don't believe that your small donation will make a difference.
- You believe that people need to solve their own problems; you pulled yourself up and therefore others need to do the same.
- You think that many other people will give, which means your time or money isn't needed.

Interestingly, affluent people tend to use a smaller percentage of their income for charitable giving than do those in lower income brackets. In the 2013 *Atlantic* article "Why the Rich Don't Give to Charity," Ken Stern speculated on why: perhaps people who live in low-income areas are more apt to see people in need, which inspires a higher level of empathy.[18]

Another possible obstacle: people identify with some causes more than others. For example, after Japan's 2011 tsunami catastrophe, Americans donated more than $700 million.[19] Although that sounds like a lot, after Hurricane Katrina struck New Orleans and surrounding areas in 2005, the donations were in the billions. Why? Because more Americans identify closely with New Orleans than with Japan. People give more generously when they feel connected to the cause. So, when considering charitable giving, look for causes that your child can connect and empathize with.

Giving back shows an appreciation of what you have. Your kid can learn that giving is important and it feels good. They learn that each of us has a responsibility to reach out and care for other people.

Some parents make the mistake of threatening donation of their child's belongings to charity as a way to punish the child: "If I don't see some appreciation from you, I'll take that toy and give it to someone who'll enjoy it." But when you use giving as punishment, you teach your child that giving is something to avoid rather than embrace.

Consider This: Tell Your Kid How You Give Back, and Why

"Parents' giving to charity is not enough to teach children to be charitable. Focused, intentional teaching by talking to children about charity is what works. This is true for children in families at all income levels and across gender, race, and age groups."[20]

— *Women Give 2013*, Lilly Family School of Philanthropy at Indiana University

---

Family Activity: What Would You Do with $1,000?

Have each person in the family imagine they were given $1,000. They were allowed to spend $500 on themselves and had to donate $500. What would they buy? How would they spend the money for charity? What made them choose the specific charities?

It Starts with a Conversation

When you give to a certain organization—in time or in dollars—let your child know. Explain why you chose this charity, and why you want to support it. Talk about times when you helped other people. Make giving commonplace: hand your child a quarter or a dollar to put into donation boxes on store counters. Work together to go through old clothes and toys to donate to Goodwill. When you make giving a part of your daily life, your child sees it as an example.

Here are some tips for talking to your child about charity and giving:

- *Look for chances to discuss ways to help solve local or world problems.* You might point out that we can help the environment by recycling, driving less, or giving money to causes that work on these issues. Look for openings to talk about life in developing countries, and how we might help families who need it. Keep your conversations age-appropriate—you don't want to scare or sadden a small child—but you want your child to be aware that the environment needs care, and that not everyone lives with the conveniences they have.

- *Read books about charitable giving.* Ellen Shabin's *The Giving Book: Open the Door to a Lifetime of Giving* is a great place to start. It helps your child appreciate other people's gifts to them: time, attention, friendship, and help, as well as presents. It then encourages children to think about ways they can give to others.

- *Engage your child's interests.* If your son loves playing baseball, he might be interested in donating money to help a child who can't afford the league fees. If he loves animals, he could donate to the local zoo or animal rescue program. Use your child's interests to show how they can make a difference in the world.

- *Talk about acts of kindness that cost nothing.* Giving back doesn't always mean giving money. It could mean cheering up someone who seems down, raking leaves for an elderly neighbor, or sharing your lunch at school.

- *Ask your child to commit to one act of kindness each day.* Work together to create a list of ideas of how to be kind. Don't forget to encourage kindness at home.

- *Discuss how it feels to give.* For most people, giving to others, whether in monetary ways or through time and effort, creates positive emotions. Focus on how your child feels when they are kind, considerate, or do something nice for someone else.

Ask your child: if they could change one thing in this world to make it a better place, what would that be? This is a good way to help your child begin to think about what charities they would like to send donations to.

Ways to Give: It's Not Just Money

Consider other ways to give through your time, effort, energy, or talents. Find what works best for you, your child, and your family. The following list provides ideas but is in no way meant to be inclusive:

- *Volunteer to clean up your local park or neighborhood.* Check with your local council or governing body to see if there is a clean-up committee. If not, consider attending a meeting and volunteering to set one up. But you don't need a committee to pick up litter or take steps to beautify your local area. Grab a trash bag and head to the park.

- *Look for fair trade products before you buy.* Fair trade signifies that the producer (either a farmer or tradesperson) was paid a fair wage, worked in safe conditions, with no social or environmental harm. While fair trade goods often cost a bit more, they help contribute to the good of the world community.

- *Volunteer your time.* Nonprofits such as VolunteerMatch .org, Idealist.org, and PointsofLight.org allow you to search for opportunities in your area that match your interests. You can also volunteer without leaving your home by making a blanket for ProjectLinus.org or putting together a box for needy families for BoxProject.org. These are good ways to get the whole family involved.

- *Go through drawers and closets* for gently used clothing, household goods, and toys. Donate at a local Goodwill store, Habitat for Humanity, family shelter, or a domestic abuse shelter.

- *Donate nonperishable foods.* Keep a basket in your kitchen and every time you go food shopping, pick up a couple extra items to add to the basket. When it's full, drop it off at a woman's shelter or check with local churches and advocacy groups in your area to see who could most benefit from it.

- *Adopt a family.* People often do this around the holidays, but you don't need to wait. Contact advocacy agencies in your area and see if there are families in need that could use help through the year. Some families have a difficult time paying for children's field trips, birthday presents, or necessities.

- *Check on elderly neighbors.* Stop by for a visit; bring dinner or a tray of cookies. Offer to go food shopping or run errands. Help with lawn care or plant a few flowers by their front door.

- *Donate blood.* This is especially important after a natural disaster but is always needed. The American Red Cross has a minimum age of seventeen, but in some states sixteen-year-olds can donate blood with parental consent.

- *Keep a donation jar in your kitchen.* Add money each time you get paid, and have your child deposit money each time they get an allowance. When the jar is full, decide together where to donate. If you can't decide on just one cause, divide the money equally among several. You might also want to set aside a portion to help survivors after a natural disaster.

- *Look for volunteer opportunities through a faith community.* Some have groups that work within the community as volunteers, or you could offer to do yard work, clean up, or other chores.

- *Visit nursing homes, veterans homes, or rehabilitation centers.* Many elderly and disabled residents in these centers don't get regular visitors. Spend an hour or two a week sitting and talking with residents.

- *Organize a book drive.* Ask neighbors, family, and friends to donate gently used books. Drop them off at a women's shelter, doctor's office, pediatric hospital, or homeless shelter.

- *Don't forget the animals.* Buy a bag of dog food and donate it to the Humane Society. While there, ask about volunteering to walk dogs or spend time with cats.

▼

KEEP CALM AND FIND A CAUSE
THAT HITS HOME

Arghh! Is your privileged kid totally uninterested in giving back, or even in learning about others less fortunate? A little stealth research might tempt them into it. If your daughter or son is crazy for soccer, for example, find an organization that brings soccer equipment to poor communities or uses soccer as a peacemaking activity in areas of conflict (search for "soccer charities," then do due diligence). Or look for a local soccer outreach group your teen could volunteer for. Through activities like this, your child will likely see and meet others with the same enthusiasm, but with much less privileged backgrounds. And then other doors may open; light bulbs may click on.

When you first raise the subject of giving back, it's natural to get some initial resistance. Your child might assume that the idea of giving means giving up something. While this might be true—they're giving time, goods, or dollars—it's not a zero-sum game. Most children (and adults) find that once they start giving, the benefits and rewards far outweigh anything they have sacrificed.

Another way to engage: find charities that offer updates to donors. (Some nonprofits, such as Save the Children, send a monthly message from the sponsored child.) Whatever the charity, ask how your child might get regular updates on what the charity is doing and how it is helping others. Keep your child involved in the process. The more they are involved, the more invested and interested they will be.

15

Declarations of Independence

FINDING YOUR WAY WITH POWER STRUGGLES

Fifteen-year-old Jonas was heading out on a Friday evening to meet friends. As he opened the front door, he turned back and said to his parents, "I'll be home by eleven." He stepped outside. His father, Doug, followed him and said, "Wait, your curfew is ten o'clock. Be home by then." Jonas replied, "Everyone else can stay out until eleven. I'm not a baby." Doug insisted on ten o'clock and stepped back inside. Jonas grumbled and kept walking.

When ten o'clock came around, Jonas wasn't home. Shortly after, Doug received a text: "Ken's car broke down. I'll be home as soon as I can." Jonas came in the door a few minutes before eleven. After a lengthy argument, Doug grounded him for a week. Throughout the week, they continued to argue about the curfew but never reached a resolution. The next time Jonas went out with friends, he had a different excuse why he was late getting home.

• • •

Power struggle, battle of the wills, mutiny on the high seas . . . call it what you will, at some point you'll probably find yourself in some kind of face-off with your son or daughter. You might get a preview in the toddler years, when children learn to say no, often with gusto. But in most families the high drama occurs in the teen years, when your child is seriously flirting with the idea of independence (even though they still need a ride to the mall). On one hand, you don't want to stifle your child's growth and genuine need for earned independence. On the other hand, it isn't fair to other family members, or yourself, for one child to break rank and dictate new terms for themselves. Yes, when the chips are down, you have the upper hand. But in fact, power struggles are a growth opportunity for your child and also for you.

What Is a Power Struggle?

"Battle of the wills" might say it best. Your child wants something—a privilege, a dispensation, a particular item—and you don't feel it is appropriate, for whatever reason. They aren't giving in. You feel stuck: you can give in to keep the peace, or you can stand your ground and risk damaging your relationship with your child.

When your child is two, three, or four and you are involved in a power struggle, the solution is simple. At this age, you do have control and you are big enough to enforce it. If your child is throwing food, you can physically remove the food. You can pick your child up, remove them from the situation, or divert their attention and know that, for most children, it will all be forgotten when something more interesting comes along. While the normal power struggles that come with this first grasp of independence can be exhausting, they aren't usually dangerous.

As children enter middle school and high school, power struggles can become more intense. Your child wants to grow up. They want to declare their independence, be their own

---

**Tip: Clear Expectations in Childhood Will
Help in the Teen Years**

Provide clear and concise expectations. Let your child know what behaviors you consider unacceptable. Let them know you won't accept abusive language, hurting others, name-calling, refusing to do chores or finish schoolwork, or mistreating their or other people's possessions—and other behaviors as you see fit. Set consequences and be consistent in following through with them. This helps establish the relationship of parental authority that you need during later adolescence.

---

person. And it's you, the parent, with your many rules, who is standing in their way. But most of the time, your child doesn't view these situations as power struggles. They believe that your rules are simply too strict, too confining, stopping them from getting what they should have (material items or, most likely, more freedom). They don't see going to a party as potentially dangerous. Their classmates are going, and therefore they should be able to go as well. Your child doesn't realize that their friends' parents are probably also calling the host's parents to find out more about the party; they only know that you want to call and are questioning their judgment. They think you are old-fashioned, or that you don't trust them.

Here's the key point: power struggles are often the result of each person looking at the situation from their own perspective only. Your teenage son sees getting a video game as harmless. His friends have the game; why can't he? You see the game as too violent or too sexualized. You look at the long-term implications of these factors because you are a parent. Your teen looks at the "right now" and doesn't understand what the big deal is. He sees you as unreasonable and stopping him from enjoying his life. The more strongly he judges your decision as unfair, the more willing he is to dig deep, stand his ground, and fight for what he wants. The challenge for both of you is to see it from the other's point of view. (This might be easier for you, because you remember what it was like to be a teen.)

Self-Reflection: What's at Stake for Me?

Power struggles are a natural part of the parent-child dynamic as the child nears adulthood. But for some parents, winning the battle of wills becomes all-important: if the parent gives in, it feels like losing control. The authoritarian mom wants her child to know she is in charge, and what she says goes. When winning a power struggle descends into an ego-driven argument, no one wins. For the parent, sometimes the best choice is not to engage. As you read on about options for handling power struggles, ask yourself what's at stake for your own ego? Challenge yourself to see it from your child's point of view.

What's a Parent to Do?

When faced with a power struggle, you might be tempted to handle it in an authoritarian style. You demand your child be respectful and follow your rules without question. Or you might tend to give in to avoid straining the relationship. It's easier to keep the peace by giving your child what they want. But both of these methods can cause further problems:

- *When you are authoritarian* and demand your child follow rules without question, they might become timid, afraid to speak up for themself, or rebel completely.

Family Activity: Self-Advocacy Skills for Teens

Create a worksheet with some basic questions about a change your teen wants implemented. If they need time to think about the answers, set up a time to talk again in a few days. Here are some questions you might ask:

- What is the change?
- Why do you want it?
- What are the benefits for you, and for us, your parents?
- How will we know the change is working?
- What are signs that it isn't working?
- What will you do if it isn't working?

Suppose your teen asks to have his bedtime changed to one hour later. They might come up with these answers:

- What is the change? *Go to bed by 11 p.m. on school nights.*
- Why do you want it? *More time to spend with my friends and still get homework done.*
- What are the benefits for you, and for us, your parents? *I get more time to talk or text with friends, and on some nights I could spend some of the extra time with you.*
- How will we know the change is working? *I get up on time in the morning, hand in homework on time, keep my grades up.*
- What are signs that it isn't working? *I'm tired during the day, grades not as good, some homework maybe doesn't get done.*
- What will you do if it isn't working? *Go to bed at 10 p.m. on school nights.*

Besides avoiding a power struggle, you've also taught them a valuable lesson in how to advocate for themself—a life skill—and provided them with a tool they can use to

— continued —

think situations through and look at the pros and cons, the risks and the benefits. You've also put responsibility for the decision in their hands. They know your expectations, so now your child wants to show you that you can trust them to make a good decision.

- *When you are permissive* and easily give in to your child's demands, you teach them that they deserve to get whatever they want, whenever they want it, even if it means bullying others.

Imagine your daughter in ten or twenty years. Suppose she has been working for a company for more than a year and thinks she deserves a raise. If she is used to accepting rules without question, she might be afraid to ask for the raise. If she intimidates others to get what she wants, she might demand the raise—and then quit if she doesn't get it, or be disciplined for her attitude.

So what's a parent to do? Ideally, you want to find some middle path, some third way, through the power struggle. And ultimately you want your child to learn to advocate for themself, properly and effectively. You do this not by quashing the dispute, but by taking the defiant attitude out of it. This way, you encourage independence in your teen while still insisting that they treat you with respect.

Three Ways to Manage Power Struggles

If your child initiates a battle of the wills—a rebellious stance against the status quo in some area of your family life—you have choices. And the right choice might depend on whether the issue is nonnegotiable, possibly negotiable, or actually quite an appropriate change, come to think of it. Let's look at each of these possible ways to respond:

1. *Avoid engaging.* If it's an issue you consider nonnegotiable —say, riding in a car driven by a friend with a revoked license—you can simply choose not to participate in the conversation. A power struggle requires that at least two people be involved. If only your child is involved, it is a tantrum. You can choose to walk away or simply not argue. Arguing tells your child you believe they have the right to challenge you on this issue. Instead, refuse to participate. Calmly state, "We've already discussed this, and I have given my answer," or "I'll be glad to talk about this later when you are calm and willing to have a discussion." Once you've made your statement, walk away. Don't engage further.

2. *Offer choices.* If there's room for compromise—say if the issue is chores—determine several choices that are acceptable to you. Let's say your teen daughter is resisting the time constraints on her tasks: living room tidied up after school every day, rugs vacuumed on Wednesday afternoons and Saturday mornings, trash to the curb by 8 p.m. Tuesdays. Lately, she's been skipping the afternoon chores because she's been making after-school plans with friends. So look for alternatives. She could straighten the living room after dinner and trade the vacuuming for cleaning the bathroom on weekends, for example. By listening to your daughter's reasoning and proposing compromises, you're showing that while chores are still mandatory, you respect that she wants to spend time with friends after school. She learns that she still must follow the rules and expectations, but if she has a compelling and reasonable proposition for change, then she has a greater chance of success in getting her needs met. You're also

modeling negotiating skills, which will serve her as she gets older.

3. *Make changes.* On some issues—weekend curfew, for example—you might actually be ready to change your policy. Your son's needs and wants change as he matures into a teenager. He will want more freedom, and you might expect him to be more responsible around the house. He might want to stay out later on the weekend or stay up later during the school week. He might want a larger allowance. When your teen makes a reasonable request in a respectful way, listen, ask questions on details that need fleshing out, and consider a change.

Resistance or Defiance?

As children grow up, they'll eventually react to your rules with some resistance. They want to learn how to live on their own, make their own rules, and set their own limits. This is to be expected. With normal-to-tough resistance, you can use the three approaches outlined above and often have good results. With defiance, however, you feel like you are pushing against a brick wall.

Defiant children refuse to follow rules. They disobey despite the consequences, or they meet your requests and demands with abusive and hurtful language. Patterns of defiance often occur, unfortunately, when parents give more attention to a child's defiant behavior than to their desired behaviors. Remember: children want attention. And any attention—including yelling, scolding, spanking, and punishing—often encourages the very behavior you want to stop. A defiant attitude—whether active or passive in tone—can lead to trouble in school, at work, in relationships, and with the legal system.

Consider This: Defiance Can Be Habit-Forming

When we allow children to express defiance, they grow up to be defiant adults. If you don't teach the lesson of respect to your child now, then the world will teach it later—and it's much harder at that point. Extended into young adulthood, defiance can result in poor academic performance, job loss, relationship problems, and divorce or legal problems.

Many children try using defiance at some point. How will it be met? That will determine whether your child decides that defiance isn't worth the trouble, or that it may actually get them what they want. Imagine the four-year-old who stubbornly stands in front of you and says, "No, I won't go to bed." If they keep it up, does defiance finally get them what they want? Does stubbornness wear you down until you let them stay up a little longer? If so, you're teaching your child that defiance works. Each time you give in, it becomes easier for your child to use it again. The urge to be defiant becomes stronger. Eventually, your child knows that if they push hard enough, they'll get their way.

Defiance can also occur in authoritarian families where parents are overly strict, tightly controlling everything their child does. These parents often veto any requests, even age-appropriate ones, because they're afraid of giving their children any independence. Children of authoritarian parents may feel the only way to gain any control over their own lives is to defy their parents' rules. They may grow into rebellious teens and eventually adults who have little regard for others. They might indulge in an addictive lifestyle or experience failure after failure because they continue to buck society's rules and expectations. Once the pattern of defiance is entrenched, it is difficult (but not impossible) to change. Children learn to use what works. If you stop giving in to defiant behavior, your child will look for a different way to get what they want. Teaching them problem-solving and self-advocacy is the best way. Some families find they need to work with a therapist or behavioral specialist, especially if these patterns have lasted for years. The therapist works both with the child on problem-solving, and with the parents on better ways to manage behavioral issues.

KEEP CALM AND FIND THE "THIRD WAY"

When it comes to teen power struggles, your own history of goodwill and generosity are like money in the bank. You've got credibility. If, over the years, you've noticed and acknowledged your child's good behavior—especially if you've mentioned it on the spot—that acknowledgement will go a long way. Your child feels appreciated, so any objections you make now deserve to be heard.

Still, your teen may push back hard against rules that feel confining. Don't take this resistance personally. It's a developmentally appropriate response in teenagers. If possible, teach self-advocacy rather than disciplining your teen. Negotiation is a life skill. Suggest that your teen offer a reasonable compromise; then negotiate. Perhaps a change could be phased in gradually. Or your teen could make a provisional plan to test an idea (see "Family Activity: Self-Advocacy Skills for Teens" earlier in this chapter). On these terms, your child is using adult skills and finding creative solutions. That third way can be eye-opening for all of you.

16

A United Front

BRINGING OTHERS ON BOARD

Children usually move through many environments as they grow up. They interact with grandparents, aunts, uncles, caregivers. In joint custody situations, they may move back and forth between parents. Even if you're doing your best to un-entitle your child, the other people in their life aren't necessarily on the same page. If others' habits with your child are a bit more indulgent, it could sabotage your efforts, however unintentionally. When that happens, not only do you have to be diligent in how you treat your child, you have to combat and possibly undo the influences of others. That may take some diplomacy.

Do Grandparents Have a Right to Spoil?

Visiting Grandma and Grandpa is a vacation, right? Rules go by the wayside, sweets are plentiful at all hours, and bedtime is a distant memory. It's a time for rules to be broken—at least some grandparents see it that way. They don't have the responsibility of your child's day-to-day care. They don't have to worry about homework. "I raised my child right. Now it's my right to spoil my grandchild," one grandmother said.

A single working mother of a seven-year-old, Elana thought having her own mom watch Jamie after school two days a week was a financial lifesaver. But after several months, Elana could tell the arrangement wasn't working. Too often, homework wasn't completed, and sometimes not even started, when she picked up her son at 6 p.m. "We were having fun playing," Elana's mother would say. "I didn't want to stop to do homework." Jamie got everything he wanted when he was with Grandmom, and it caused problems at home, where Elana's standards were stricter. She wanted Jamie to appreciate the toys he already owned, but every week Grandmom had a new toy for Jamie, despite Elana's requests not to.

One week, Jamie greeted Elana at her mother's door with a hug. "Grandmom bought me a new stuffed animal!" Elana's annoyance quickly turned to anger when her mother said, "I know you aren't going to like this, but Jamie just loved it and I didn't want to disappoint him." It was a stuffed bear that belched when you pressed its belly. Her mother was right; Elana didn't like it. In fact, she found it obnoxious and couldn't wait to throw it away. After that, she decided the money spent on daily after-school care was a priority. Jamie still saw his grandmother regularly, but only when Elana was with him.

Usually, a grandparent's spoiling doesn't interfere with your parenting. At a young age, children learn that different behaviors are okay at different places. They know that at a worship service they sit quietly, at school they stay at their desk during class, in a library they whisper, at recess they can run and use outdoor voices, and at home they can play and use indoor voices. Most of the time, children quickly adapt to their circumstances and adjust their behavior accordingly. Even if they don't understand the reason, they know they can get away with certain behaviors at grandmom's house that they couldn't at home.

But sometimes there's a transition time when you must remind them where they are and what you expect of them. When this transition time makes home life difficult or if it extends too long, it's time to set limits on your parents or in-laws interactions with your child—starting with setting clear expectations and, if that doesn't work, by limiting time spent together.

Here are some ideas to help you address the situation:

- *Make plans to talk with your relatives when your child isn't with you.* Start by expressing your appreciation—for how they raised you, how much they love your child, that they help with child care or take your child overnight to give you a break. Then enlist their help by explaining a specific way their behavior is harmful to your child. For example, "Jamie has trouble settling down to do homework when we wait until 7 p.m. to get started. I am worried that he'll fall behind. Do you think you could make sure his homework is done before I pick him up?" You'll probably get a more positive response if you frame it as supporting your efforts rather than criticizing their efforts.

- *Set guidelines for gifts.* Some examples include:
  - Before buying gifts over a certain dollar amount, you want them to talk to you first.
  - Any new toys bought must stay at their house.
  - Set limits, such as one small purchase (less than ten dollars) each month instead of one each visit.
  - Have your child do a few chores at their house before receiving a gift or money.

- *Remind your relatives that spending time together is what counts.* Your child has probably told you about activities they have done with their grandparents—maybe going to the park or a day at the zoo. Let your parents know that their grandchild has talked about their adventures and these times mean much more to your child than receiving a toy.

- *Overlook small spoils.* Your mother might let your child have soda with dinner even though you insist on milk at home. On overnights, your in-laws might let your child stay up later than you would. Keep your perspective when considering which actions need discussing and which you can let slide.

There might be times when talking doesn't seem to help. If your relatives seem to be undermining your authority as a parent or you believe your child's health or safety is at risk—for example, they're not paying attention to food allergies or not using a car seat—you must be more forceful in your approach. At these times, it is important to set limitations and rules. "Jamie must always ride in a car seat. If you can't follow that rule, I cannot have him come here except when I am visiting with you." Or "Jamie can't have dairy products. I will be glad to give you some alternatives, such as soy milk, but if you continue to give him dairy products, he won't be able to visit after school anymore."

Co-parents: Try for Consistent Messages

Co-parenting is hard even when you and your ex are on friendly terms. Chances are, both of you have different perspectives on parenting and running a household. Both of you are going through different emotions regarding the divorce and parenting. Often, one parent spoils the child with grand adventures, money, or gifts. Even when unintentional, this can interfere with daily parenting.

> Twelve-year-old Randy wanted a cell phone, but his mom, Erin, thought he was too young. She told him she'd consider it on his next birthday, but first he needed to improve his grades at school. A month later, at his dad's house for the weekend, Randy mentioned wanting a phone. His dad, Carl, took him out to buy one and added him to his plan. Erin was angry. This wasn't the first time she'd felt blindsided. Randy often came home on Sunday evening still needing to finish the homework he'd brought with him to Carl's. Randy often spent those weekends playing Carl's video games. Other times, they went on overnight trips. Erin thought Carl was spoiling Randy.

To many divorced parents, it might seem as if the other parent spoils your child to undermine you, make you look bad, or just to elevate themselves in their child's eyes. They might believe the other parent does so selfishly, not thinking about the aftereffects or the long-term consequences. This isn't necessarily the case. When a divorced parent spoils their child, they may do so out of guilt or they might want to make the little time they spend together memorable. They might want to avoid conflict during short visits and overcompensate by being more permissive. Often, it isn't done with malice or bad intentions; it is done because of feelings of inadequacy for not being there on a daily basis.

No matter the reason, the other parent (often the custodial parent) must deal with the aftermath. They have to be the disciplinarian, the "mean" parent, the one that enforces the rules and says no. Although it doesn't seem fair, it is often a part of divorce.

Tip: Keep Your Authority in Your Home

It's important for your child's well-being for you to retain your authority in your own home without undermining your ex's authority in theirs. When Randy came home with a cell phone before Erin believed he was ready, she could have responded, "That is great that your father bought you this. But you understand the rule in this house is not until your next birthday. In the meantime, you can use it at your father's house if that is his rule. At this house, it will be put away until your birthday." Once you decide on your position, let your ex know. Explain that you are not trying to undermine their authority in their house, but that you expect your child to follow your rules in your house.

The following ideas might help:

- *Talk to your co-parent about your concerns.* When you do, don't be accusatory or make demands. You can make suggestions, but your ex is not obligated to follow them. Explain how you think this is affecting your child, for example, say, "Dylan is expected to do chores at home before he receives an allowance; however, when you send him home with money, he believes he doesn't need to do them." Then ask your ex to work with you. Ask for their suggestions on how you can work together to solve the problem.

- *Clarify that different households have different rules.* For example, your child might not need to complete chores at his mother's house but must do so at yours. Explain the expectations and consequences for your household and keep your comments regarding expectations at your co-parent's house to yourself.

- *Encourage gratitude for anything received from the co-parent.* Entitlement comes from a belief that you deserve things and favors simply because you are you. Remind your child that they should be appreciative rather than believing they deserve material items, money, or trips.

- *Avoid trying to outdo your co-parent.* If your child is always coming home telling you about grand adventures, the luxuries they have at your ex's house, or about the money and gifts their other parent gave them, you might feel intimidated or insecure. Remember that your child loves both of you. You don't need to try to outdo one another.

Non-family Caregivers: Find a Healthy Balance

Of all the outside influencers who can spoil your child, non-relative paid caregivers are the easiest to manage. You have control over who cares for your child. You have the right to

---

Parent Challenge: Set Some Common Standards

Talk to your ex about the general rules in that household. Be sure to explain that you aren't judging but are looking for a few common rules that you can both post in your homes to find common ground. These might include that your child:

- starts homework right after school
- has one hour of screen time on school nights
- goes to bed by 8:30 p.m.
- always places their dishes in the sink after eating
- is courteous to everyone

Write the rules on a white board in both houses to remind your child that some expectations are the same in both homes, although other rules may vary.

---

change caregivers if you aren't satisfied with the care your child is receiving or if the caregiver isn't following your rules or consistently ignores your instructions. Constantly changing caregivers, however, isn't healthy for your child.

These tips may help you better work with caregivers:

- *Use clear communication.* When you have a caregiver or babysitter come to your home, write down your routines and house rules. Be specific on rules where you don't want to allow flexibility, such as only one hour of screen time at night. If you have rules you want followed exactly and others where you are more flexible, let the babysitter know.

- *Remember the caregiver's main responsibilities* are to keep your child safe, supervise and interact with them, and treat them lovingly. While you want the babysitter to follow your instructions, you also want to provide enough freedom to let their relationship develop.

- *Keep your expectations realistic.* Your babysitter is not going to do everything exactly as you do it. It is emotionally healthy for your child to see and interact with different people.

- *Explain your discipline process.* If you use a specific chair for a time-out, let the babysitter know. If you prefer your child go to their room, share that information. If you prefer your child go to bed earlier than normal for certain behaviors, explain what those would be.

If you must discuss a problem with your caregiver, never do so in front of your child. This undermines your caregiver's authority and may make their job more difficult in the future.

We all spoil our children from time to time. We might indulge them by allowing them to stay up a little later than usual or buying a special treat from the store. These occasional indulgences can be beneficial, letting your child know they are important. The same is true for extended family members. There isn't anything wrong with allowing them to spoil your child from time to time. When this behavior becomes disruptive to your family life, however, or is in direct opposition to the values you are trying to instill in your child or undermines your authority as a parent, you need to address it.

KEEP CALM—EVEN WHEN YOUR CHILD BRINGS HOME A BELCHING TEDDY BEAR

Remember the belching teddy bear Elana's mom bought even after Elana had specifically asked her mother to skip any further gifts. Later, Elana found a quiet moment to ditch the bear (not wanting to wish it on a Goodwill shopper). But how can Elana get through to her mother about this issue?

When talking to family members about spoiling your child, try to address your concerns by explaining how the behavior negatively affects your *child* in the long run. Place the emphasis on your child, rather than on yourself and your rules.

Always keep your expectations realistic. No one, not even your partner, is going to treat your child exactly as you do. That is a good thing. You want your child to experience many different types of personalities and develop good interpersonal skills. Before criticizing how other people treat your child, make sure it's a legitimate issue with some stakes—not just a matter of style.

— *continued* —

Remind family members that spending time together and showing love are more valuable than material items. Years from now, your child probably won't remember a toy their grandparents bought when they were young, but your child will always remember spending time with them.

Afterword

Congratulations on taking the first step toward raising a confident, responsible, kind, and caring child.

As you have adopted some of the strategies in this book, you might have seen your child react negatively. That is to be expected. You are changing the status quo in your family, and they want it to remain the same. They're going to push back and buck the changes. They might lash out, tell you they hate you, yell, or act out.

Keep it up! Stick with the new patterns you've started. Your kid's resistance lets you know that you're on the right track. Your response should be consistent. You've decided what behaviors you find acceptable and which ones you won't tolerate (at least not without consequences). Now you need to hold firm. Keep in mind that you are demanding a positive change that will benefit your child for the rest of their life. It is better that they learn these lessons now, when change is easier, rather than when they are adults and the world is less forgiving.

The strategies and techniques in this book will help to change and shape your child's character. By instilling a sense of responsibility, accountability, kindness, and caring, you are giving your child the skills they need to lead a happy and productive life. Life isn't going to always be easy, and change isn't going to happen overnight. It might have taken you years to get to this point, and it might take years to fully break the cycle of entitlement in your home. But once you truly change yourself, your expectations, and your reactions, your child will change as well. It's up to you.

You might hear other parents say, "I can't believe I turned out just like my mother (or my father). All those years ago, when I was young I said I wouldn't be the same kind of parent, but here I am, saying the same things they did." Such observations are a testament to parents' great influence over their children's adult lives. What we think, what we expect, and what we demand greatly influences our children throughout their lives.

If you believe your child is entitled, or headed that way, it is time to take charge. It is time to be the adult. This book is a good start, but it is just the first leg on your journey. Keep it handy to refer to it as your child grows and matures. Write notes in the margins; dog-ear the pages you find most helpful; read and reread it. As your child grows and new dynamics arise, revisit the tips and the family activities to find those that apply. The more worn-out this book is, the more you are using the strategies and making changes. Refer back to it often. Your child will be better off because of your efforts.

Keep calm and change on.

Acknowledgments

Eileen Bailey and Dr. Michael Wetter would like to thank our agent, Marilyn Allen, for her unwavering belief in us. We also would like to thank the editing team at Hazelden Publishing, including Vanessa Torrado, Mindy Keskinen, and the many others who worked diligently to make this book a reality.

Eileen: I would also like to thank Dr. Michael Wetter for continuing to be a wonderful co-author. It is always a pleasure to work with Michael. Writing this book, while dealing with my son's illness over the past year and his death in January 2017, was extremely difficult at times. I would like to express my deepest gratitude to Michael, the editing team at Hazelden, and the many wonderful relatives and friends who offered tremendous support. My sister, Kathi Shetty, is due a multitude of thanks for everything she did to help me in managing my son's illness. And, of course, thanks to my son, Derek, for being exactly who you were, a kind and generous soul. I miss you every day.

Michael: I would like to acknowledge and thank Eileen Bailey for continuing to be the best part of their collaborative "dream team" writing partnership. I look forward to our continued collaboration on many more topics to come; you are a singular talent and trusted partner. I would also like to express my most sincere appreciation to my family, friends, and peers who continue to offer unyielding support in my efforts. Finally, I would like to acknowledge my late grandparents Blanche and Irving Wetter, and Hinda and Saul Slotow. As survivors of the Holocaust, they demonstrated that the enduring qualities of love, courage, and kindness far exceed the shallow value of entitlement—a lesson, I pray, that continues to be practiced for generations to come.

Notes

1. Jean Twenge, *Generation Me: Why Today's Young Americans Are More Confident, Assertive, Entitled—and More Miserable Than Ever Before* (New York: Atria Books, 2014), 17.

2. Eddie Brummelman et al., "Origins of Narcissism in Children," *Proceedings of the National Academy of Sciences* 112, no. 12 (March 24, 2015): 3659–3662, www.pnas.org/content/112/12/3659.short.

3. Igor Grossman and Michael E. W. Varnum, "Social Structure, Infectious Diseases, Disasters, Secularism, and Cultural Change in America," *Psychological Science* 26, no. 3 (2015), http://journals.sagepub.com/doi/abs/10.1177/0956797614563765.

4. Tim Henderson, "Growing Number of People Living Solo Can Pose Challenges," *Stateline*, September 11, 2014, www.pewtrusts.org/en/research-and-analysis/blogs/stateline/2014/09/11/growing-number-of-people-living-solo-can-pose-challenges.

5. Paula Gardner (psychologist, Southern Columbia Area School District, Catawissa, PA), personal interview, November 5, 2016.

6. Ellen Greenberger et al., "Self-Entitled College Students: Contributions of Personality, Parenting, and Motivational Factors," *Journal of Youth and Adolescence* 37, no. 10 (November 2008): 1193–1204, www.westernu.edu/bin/ime/greenberger-academic-entitlement.pdf.

7. James Harrison (linebacker, Pittsburgh Steelers), Instagram post, August 15, 2015, www.instagram.com/p/6aXCJ2JFi5/?hl=en.

8. American Academy of Pediatrics, Committee on Communications, "Children, Adolescents and Advertising," *Pediatrics* 118, no. 6 (December 2006), http://pediatrics.aappublications.org/content/118/6/2563.

9. Michael David Smith, "Fernando Bryant Fired by High School over Social Media Post," NBC Sports, February 23, 2017, http://profootballtalk.nbcsports.com/2017/02/23/fernando-bryant-fired-by-high-school-over-social-media-post.

10. Robert A. Emmons, *Thanks! How the New Science of Gratitude Can Make You Happier* (New York: Houghton Mifflin Harcourt, 2007), 11.

11. J. J. Froh, W. J. Sefick, and R. A. Emmons, "Counting Blessings in Early Adolescents: An Experimental Study of Gratitude and Subjective Well-Being," *Journal of School Psychology* 46, no. 2 (April 2008): 213–233, www.ncbi.nlm.nih.gov/pubmed/19083358.

12. American Psychological Association, "Growing Up Grateful Gives Teens Multiple Mental Health Benefits, New Research Shows," press release, August 5, 2012, www.apa.org/news/press/releases/2012/08/health -benefits.aspx.

13. Amber J. Hammons and Barbara H. Fiese, "Is Frequency of Shared Family Meals Related to Nutritional Health of Children and Adolescents?," *Pediatrics* 127, no. 6 (June 2011), http://pediatrics .aappublications.org/content/127/6/e1565.

14. Philanthropy News Digest, "18 Percent of Americans Familiar with 'Giving Tuesday,' Survey Finds," November 26, 2015, http:// philanthropynewsdigest.org/news/18-percent-of-americans-familiar -with-giving-tuesday-survey-finds.

15. Rick Weissbourd, Stephanie Jones, et al., *The Children We Mean to Raise: The Real Messages Adults Are Sending About Values* (Cambridge, MA: Harvard Graduate School of Education, 2014).

16. Marie-Anne Suizzo, "Parents' Goals and Values for Children," *Journal of Cross-Cultural Psychology* 38, no. 4 (July 1, 2007): 506–503, http://journals.sagepub.com/doi/abs/10.1177/0022022107302365? journalCode=jcca.

17. Cyberbullying Research Center, *2016 Cyberbullying Statistics*, http://cyberbullying.org/2016-cyberbullying-data.

18. Ken Stern, "Why the Rich Don't Give to Charity," *The Atlantic*, April 2013, www.theatlantic.com/magazine/archive/2013/04 /why-the-rich-dont-give/309254/.

19. Tom Paulson, "Why Did Americans Donate $730 Million to Wealthy Japan?" *Humanosphere*, March 11, 2014, www.humanosphere .org/basics/2014/03/why-americans-donated-730-million-to-aid -japan-after-quake-tsunami/.

20. Debra Mesch and Una Osili, *Women Give 2013: New Research on Charitable Giving by Girls and Boys* (Indianapolis: University of Indiana, Lilly Family School of Philanthropy, 2016), 15, https://philanthropy .iupui.edu/files/research/women_give_2013-final9-12-2013.pdf.

Bibliography

American Psychological Association. "Growing Up Grateful Gives Teens Multiple Mental Health Benefits," *Science Daily*, August 6, 2012. www.sciencedaily.com/releases/2012/08/120806093938.htm.

Business Wire. "New Study Reveals Staggering Number of Americans Contributing to Holiday Consumerism," November 23, 2015. www.businesswire.com/news/home/20151123005345/en/Study -Reveals-Staggering-Number-Americans-Contributing-Holiday.

D'Amico, James V. *The Affluenza Antidote: How Wealthy Families Can Raise Grounded Children in an Age of Apathy and Entitlement*. CreateSpace Independent Publishing Platform, 2010.

DeAngelis, Tori. "Class Differences." *Monitor on Psychology* 46, no. 2 (February 2015): 62. www.apa.org/monitor/2015/02/class-differences .aspx.

Deerwester, Karen. *The Entitlement-Free Child: Raising Confident and Responsible Kids in a "Me, Mine, Now!" Culture*. Naperville, IL: Sourcebooks, Inc., 2009.

Doherty, William J. *Take Back Your Kids: Confident Parenting in Turbulent Times*. Notre Dame, IN: Sorin Books, 2000.

Eyre, Richard, and Linda Eyre. *The Entitlement Trap: How to Rescue Your Child with a New Family System of Choosing, Earning, and Ownership*. New York: Avery, 2011.

Freind, Chris. "Millennials' Entitlement Attitude Must Be Rejected." *Newsmax* (April 16, 2015), www.newsmax.com/Freind/Duke -University/2015/04/16/id/638992.

Fry, Carla, and Lisa Ferrari. *Gratitude and Kindness: A Modern Parents Guide to Raising Children in an Era of Entitlement*. Real Parenting Lab, 2015.

Holdcroft, Barbara. "Student Incivility, Intimidation, and Entitlement in Academia," *Academe*, May–June 2014. www.aaup.org/article/student -incivility-intimidation-and-entitlement-academia#.WJzOBYWcEjx.

Indiana University–Purdue University Indianapolis. "How Parents Teach Children About Charitable Giving Matters, New Study Finds," September 12, 2013. http://news.iupui.edu/releases/2013/09/children -charitable-study.shtml.

Johnson, Emma. "Best Charity Sites to Teach Kids About Giving," *Forbes*, February 26, 2015. www.forbes.com/sites/emmajohnson/2015/02/26 /best-charity-sites-to-teach-kids-about-giving/#4673c3d57023.

Kapp, Diana. "Raising Children with an Attitude of Gratitude," *The Wall Street Journal*, December 23, 2013. www.wsj.com/articles/SB10001424052702 303773704579270293660965768.

Kohn, Alfie. *The Myth of the Spoiled Child: Challenging the Conventional Wisdom about Children and Parenting.* Philadelphia: Da Capo Press, 2014.

Manne, Anne. "The Age of Entitlement: How Wealth Breeds Narcissism," *The Guardian*, July 7, 2014. www.theguardian.com/commentisfree/2014 /jul/08/the-age-of-entitlement-how-wealth-breeds-narcissism.

Moorman, Chick and Thomas Haller. "9 Ways to Teach Your Child about Charity," *Parent*, undated. www.parents.com/parenting/money /donate-to-charity/9-ways-to-teach-your-child-about-charity-/.

Oneill, Therese. "11 Lessons Every Good Parent Should Teach Their Kid," *The Week*, June 18, 2014. http://theweek.com/articles/446231/11 -lessons-every-good-parent-should-teach-kid.

Patton, Stacey. "Dear Student: No, I Won't Change the Grade You Deserve," *ChronicleVitae*, February 13, 2015. https://chroniclevitae.com/news /908-dear-student-no-i-won-t-change-the-grade-you-deserve.

Szalavitz, Maia. "Wealthy Selfies: How Being Rich Increases Narcissism," *Time Magazine*, August 20, 2013. http://healthland.time.com/2013 /08/20/wealthy-selfies-how-being-rich-increases-narcissism.

Welch, Kristen. *Raising Grateful Kids in an Entitled World: How One Family Learned That Saying No Can Lead to Life's Biggest Yes.* Carol Stream, IL: Tyndale Momentum, 2016.

Woollaston, Victoria. "Think the 'Me Me Me Generation' Is New? Think Again: Society Began Shifting Towards Individualism More Than a CENTURY Ago," *Daily Mail*, February 6, 2015. www.dailymail.co.uk /sciencetech/article-2942561/Think-Generation-new-Think-Society -began-shifting-individualism-CENTURY-ago.html.

Wyma, Kay Wills. *Cleaning House: A Mom's Twelve-Month Experiment to Rid Her Home of Youth Entitlement.* Colorado Springs: WaterBrook, 2012.

About the Authors

Dr. Michael G. Wetter is a licensed clinical psychologist specializing in adolescent and adult populations.  He has served on the faculty and staff of several leading national medical organizations including Kaiser Permanente and Cedars–Sinai Medical Center. A subject matter expert for the California Board of Psychology, Dr. Wetter is also a nationally recognized expert in the field of psychology. He has served as an expert consultant on numerous television programs as well as to newspapers such as the *Washington Post, Boston Globe*, and *Atlanta Journal–Constitution* and magazines such as *Men's Health, Forbes, Prevention*, and *Redbook*. He is the coauthor (with Eileen Bailey) of *What Went Right: Reframe Your Thinking for a Happier Now.* Dr. Wetter lives with his family in Los Angeles, where he maintains his private clinical practice.

Eileen Bailey is a freelance writer specializing in mental and emotional health issues. She writes for numerous health and wellness websites. For HealthCentral.com, she writes on anxiety and is lead writer on attention deficit-hyperactivity disorder.  A contributing writer for *ADDitude Magazine* online, she has also coauthored five previous books: *What Went Right: Reframe Your Thinking for a Happier Now* (with Michael Wetter), *The Complete Idiot's Guide to Adult ADHD, Idiot's Guides: Cognitive Behavioral Therapy, The Essential Guide to Overcoming Obsessive Love*, and *The Essential Guide to Asperger's Syndrome.*

About Hazelden Publishing

As part of the Hazelden Betty Ford Foundation, Hazelden Publishing offers both cutting-edge educational resources and inspirational books. Our print and digital works help guide individuals in treatment and recovery, and their loved ones. Professionals who work to prevent and treat addiction also turn to Hazelden Publishing for evidence-based curricula, digital content solutions, and videos for use in schools, treatment programs, correction programs, and electronic health records systems. We also offer training for implementation of our curricula.

Through published and digital works, Hazelden Publishing extends the reach of healing and hope to individuals, families, and communities affected by addiction and related issues.

For more information about Hazelden publications,
please call **800-328-9000**
or visit us online at **hazelden.org/bookstore**.

OTHER TITLES THAT MAY INTEREST YOU:

What Went Right
Reframe Your Thinking for a Happier Now
MICHAEL G. WETTER, PSYD, AND EILEEN BAILEY

Learn to change the self-critical stories in your mind and reframe your perception to gain the self-confidence needed to build a more fulfilling relationship, career, and social life. Through practical, easy-to-understand principles and techniques, as well as real-life examples, *What Went Right* teaches you to recognize and intervene on self-defeating thought processes.

Order No. 9610 (softcover), EB9610 (ebook)

It Takes a Family
A Cooperative Approach to Lasting Sobriety
DEBRA JAY

Most books on recovery from addiction focus on either the addict or the family. While most alcoholics and addicts coming out of treatment have a recovery plan, families are often left to figure things out for themselves. In *It Takes a Family*, Debra Jay takes a fresh approach to the recovery process by making family members and friends part of the recovery team, beginning in the early stages of sobriety.

Order No. 7559 (softcover), EB7559 (ebook)

Today's Gift
Daily Meditations for Families

The meditations in this book nurture family esteem, strengthen family bonds, and help readers consider topics like harmony, sharing, individuality, trust, privacy, and tolerance.

Order No. 1031 (softcover), EB1031 (ebook)